Whitewashing War

Historical Myth, Corporate Textbooks, and Possibilities for Democratic Education

Whitewashing War

Historical Myth, Corporate Textbooks, and Possibilities for Democratic Education

CHRISTOPHER R. LEAHEY

Foreword by E. Wayne Ross

Teachers College, Columbia University
New York and London

Published by Teachers College Press, 1234 Amsterdam Avenue, New York, NY 10027

Library of Congress Cataloging-in-Publication Data

Leahey, Christopher R.
  Whitewashing war : historical myth, corporate textbooks, and possibilities for democratic education / Christopher R. Leahey ; foreword by E. Wayne Ross.
      p. cm.
  Includes bibliographical references and index.
  ISBN 978-0-8077-5043-8 (pbk. : alk. paper)
  ISBN 978-0-8077-5044-5 (hardcover : alk. paper)
    1. Vietnam War, 1961–1975—Study and teaching—United States.
  2. Vietnam War, 1961–1975—Historiography. 3. Textbooks—Political aspects—United States. 4. Textbook bias—United States. 5. Myth—Political aspects—United States. 6. Education—Political aspects—United States. 7. War and education—United States. I. Title.
  DS557.74.L43 2010
  959.704'3071073—dc22   2009033724

ISBN 978-0-8077-5043-8 (paperback)
ISBN 978-0-8077-5044-5 (hardcover)

Printed on acid-free paper
Manufactured in the United States of America

17 16 15 14 13 12 11 10   8 7 6 5 4 3 2 1

For Ava, Ian, and Ryan,
who bring me so much joy and laughter

Contents

Foreword

In his introduction to *Whitewashing War*, Chris Leahey provides us with a brief account of what it was like to teach 9th-grade social studies in 2003, during the time leading up to the Iraq war. His students were curious and inquisitive about the causes and rationales for going to war. Meanwhile, the mainstream media acted as a mouthpiece for the neoconservative insiders, ignoring the social, political, and economic antecedents of the conflict along with any international and anti-war perspectives, and accepting at face value what turned out to be the Bush administration's lies created to justify the invasion of Iraq (Lewis & Reading-Smith, 2008).

What is a social studies teacher to do under such circumstances? *Whitewashing War* initiates a discussion about how we teach about American wars. Leahey's critical analysis of history textbook accounts of the Vietnam War will surely stimulate that conversation, while providing readers with compelling insights into history teaching and curriculum. The relevance of Leahey's analysis with regard to how we think and teach about the current wars in Iraq and Afghanistan is crystal clear. *Whitewashing War* compels readers to reckon with how schools in general, and the social studies curriculum in particular, can be seen as instruments of social control. Indeed, Leahey's analysis shares much in common with Hermann and Chomsky's (1988) propaganda model, which asserts that the media—history curriculum in this case—creates necessary illusions that reflect the consensus of the powerful elites of the state-corporate nexus.

As I have written with my colleague Rich Gibson, any nation promising perpetual war on the world is likely to make peculiar demands on its schools and impositions on its teachers and youth (Gibson & Ross, 2009). I believe the primary role of capitalist schooling is social control, manipulating the poor and working classes to be loyal, obedient, dutiful, and useful to the ruling classes under a variety of myths: We are all in this together; This is a multicultural society; Democracy trumps inequality; Anyone can be President; etc.

Schools serve to train the next generation of workers and school-ing is increasingly divided along razor sharp lines—from pre-prison schooling in some urban and rural areas, to pre-military schooling, to pre–middle-class teacher training, to pre-med or pre-law, to the private school systems of the rich. Schools do skills training and, depend-ing on where a child is, some limited intellectual training. In public schools the key issues of life—work, production and reproduction, ra-tional knowledge, and freedom—are virtually illegal.

It is illegal in California, for example, to teach positive things about the communist movement, and hence nearly impossible to teach about unionism. When talking about religion, educators are forbidden from presenting multiple perspectives on the existence of God, and any critique of religion or faith is prohibited. And many visitors to any school will quickly perceive that "freedom" is a sheer abstraction in the classroom, as the system of school surveillance (both physical and intellectual) is carefully designed to eradicate thinking for oneself.

Nevertheless, it is true that schools fashion hope, real or false, and that societies that erase hope are commonly steeped in rebellion (e.g., France in 1968). Redesigning "hope" and tamping down expectations of school workers, parents, and kids, is often considered the true result of the No Child Left Behind project. The current education agenda came into being after the ruling classes nearly lost control of schools and universities after the Vietnam War was lost. That agenda can be summarized by: (1) the regimentation of curricula (phonics, abstract math, the eradication of historic truths and academic freedom); (2) racist and anti–working-class high-stakes examinations; and (3) the deepening militarization of schooling. The education agenda is indeed a war agenda (Gibson & Ross, 2009; Ross & Gibson, 2007; Saltman & Gabbard, 2003).

While millions of people hit the streets to protest the invasion of Iraq in 2003, since then the anti-war movement in the United States has largely been a failure. Most anti-war activity in the past 2 years was aimed at electing Barack Obama, who ironically was more open and honest than many of his liberal and leftist backers would have liked in proclaiming that he had every intention of sustaining and expanding the empire's wars. But, more importantly, the anti-war movement failed to take up the pedagogical and practical tasks at hand: *teaching people how to develop strategy and tactics for action—working within specific com-munities and rooted in rational answers about why things are as they are.*

The crowning achievement of *Whitewashing War* is that it clearly illustrates the necessity of pursuing rational answers about why things are as they are (or were as they were). It becomes clear upon reading this book that, if we help our students pursue rational answers in the course of creating personally meaningful understandings of the world, they will figure out just what it is that needs to be done.

—E. Wayne Ross, University of British Columbia

REFERENCES

Gibson, R., & Ross, E. W. (2009). The education agenda is a war agenda: Connecting reason to power and power to resistance. *Workplace: A Journal for Academic Labor, 15*. Retrieved August 31, 2009, from http://m1.cust.educ.ubc.ca/journal/index.php/workplace/article/view/47

Hermann, E. S., & Chomsky, N. (1988). *Manufacturing consent: The political economy of the mass media*. New York: Pantheon.

Lewis, C., & Reading-Smith, M. (2008). False pretenses. *The war card: Orchestrated deception on the path to war*. Washington, DC: The Center for Public Integrity. Retrieved August 31, 2009, from http://projects.publicintegrity.org/WarCard/

Ross, E. W., & Gibson, R. (2007). *Neoliberalism and education reform*. Cresskill, NJ: Hampton Press.

Saltman, K. J., & Gabbard, D. (2003). *Education as enforcement: The militarization and corporatization of schooling*. New York: RoutledgeFalmer.

Acknowledgments

In writing this book I have incurred a number of academic and personal debts. This study began as my dissertation at the State University of New York at Binghamton. I must thank Larry Stedman, my advisor and the chair of my committee. Larry provided assistance in planning, writing, and editing my thesis, the basis of this book. An accomplished scholar and gifted teacher, Larry is a professor who has the talent and patience to support graduate students in generating quality research. I also acknowledge E. Wayne Ross, a curricular theorist who taught me that political struggle is an inherent part of public education. Wayne's passion for public education and dedication to social justice inspired this project. I am also grateful to Dr. James Carpenter, a former social studies teacher and professor, who encouraged me to write about my classroom experiences, and to historian John Stoner, whose keen eye for detail and familiarity with Cold War history greatly improved this project.

I also express my gratitude to two distinguished Vietnam War historians who took the time to review my work. Fredrik Logevall, an expert on the political landscape that surrounded the Gulf of Tonkin crisis, made suggestions concerning historical sources that greatly improved my understanding of the political decisions that led to U.S. escalation. Ed Moise, an authority on the Gulf of Tonkin crisis, made valuable recommendations on interpretation, use of historical evidence, and documentation that greatly improved Chapter 3. In addition, I would like to acknowledge Marie Ellen Larcada, senior acquisitions editor, and Karl Nyberg, senior production editor, at Teachers College Press, who made the publication of this project possible. I alone am solely responsible for this project's interpretations, arguments, conclusions, and shortcomings.

I am especially indebted to a number of family and friends who supported this work. My parents, Richard and Janet Bresnahan, and my brother, William Leahey, offered words of encouragement throughout the writing process. My sister, Tricia Leahey, a young scholar, was supportive and made helpful suggestions for improving Chapter 4. I also thank my colleagues, Steve Cary and James Schlotzhauer, for the rich discussions about history education and classroom teaching.

I would be remiss not to thank my wife and best friend, Heather. She has been a constant source of inspiration and encouragement. Without her continuous support, countless contributions, and sacrifices, this project would not have been possible. And finally, I acknowledge my beloved distractions, Ava, Ian, and Ryan, all born at different stages of this project. They teach me that play must sometimes precede work. Their love and affection sustained me through the rigors of researching, writing, and revising this book.

Introduction

This book was inspired by questions raised by high school students during the months leading up to the United States' 2003 invasion of Iraq. At that time I was teaching 9th-grade history in a suburb of Syracuse, New York. As my 9th-grade students asked salient questions about the causes of the conflict and the possibility for war, I decided to have them examine how their local media captured the impending conflict. Throughout our 3-week classroom study, students were interested in learning about the Iraqi people, American political and economic motivations for war, and the prospects for peace. After critically examining the Syracuse *Post Standard*'s coverage of the conflict, many students were dismayed to find that their local media did not cover the social, political, and economic antecedents of the conflict, ignored international perspectives and voices of dissent, and focused on hawkish statements made by American military and political leaders (Leahey, 2004).

Broader analyses supported our conclusions about the media's cursory treatment of the conflict. A Fairness & Accuracy in Reporting (FAIR) examination of the first 3 weeks of nightly news coverage of the war found that "viewers were more than six times as likely to see a pro-war source as one who was anti-war" (Rendall & Broughel, 2003, para. 4). Not only was the media failing to offer a balanced depiction of the conflict, the White House was actively using the media as a conduit for misinformation. A Center for Public Integrity report shows that in the 2 years preceding the 2003 invasion, key members of the Bush Administration made 935 false statements about the threat posed by Saddam Hussein and Iraq's weapons program (The Center for Public Integrity, 2008, para. 1).

At this critical time in American history the media failed to challenge the Bush Administration's pronouncements, seek out alternative sources of information, provide space for dissenting voices, and portray the dangers and complexity of war. Rather than challenging official statements and seeking out alternative sources of information, the American media effectively promoted the war. For instance, just hours before the March 20th invasion, major news outlets began depicting the looming war as a spectacle. MSNBC ran "Countdown Iraq," an electronic clock showing the hours Saddam Hussein had to comply with President Bush's directive to leave Iraq. By prefacing its half-hour segments with the slogan "Showdown: Iraq," CNN treated the pending invasion as a Western gunfight. NBC's "Target Iraq," CBS's "America at War," and NBC's "War in Iraq" packaged the crises as a commodity to be consumed, not as a critical event worthy of a national discourse.

As I watched events unfold, it became evident that the Bush Administration was using the media to build and maintain public support for the war. Shortly after the invasion, the Pentagon sensationalized the rescue of Private Jessica Lynch. This was later made into a melodramatic NBC TV movie, *Saving Jessica Lynch* (a transparent play on the patriotic *Saving Private Ryan*). A week later the Pentagon released a staged video of Iraqi citizens celebrating as the U.S. military toppled a statue of Saddam Hussein. This spectacle was followed by President Bush's premature May 1 declaration that all major combat operations were officially ended.

The media's war coverage and the Bush Administration's misinformation campaign highlight the importance of critically examining the media. These issues present challenges to social studies educators charged with preparing students for participatory government. As teachers, do we deviate from our prescribed state curricula? If so, how much time should be spent on recent events? What approach should we take? Thus far, little has been done to shed light on these questions. Although the National Council for Social Studies (NCSS) has crafted position statements on issues like intelligent design, sexism, and the *No Child Left Behind Act*, it has failed to construct a statement articulating its position on the war. This is disturbing when teachers like Michael Baker, Alberto Gutierrez, and Deborah Mayer have been disciplined or fired for teaching about or openly opposing the wars in Afghanistan and Iraq. (Baker, a senior social studies teacher at Lincoln, Nebraska's East High, was fired for showing his geography class *Baghdad ER*, which chronicles life inside a combat support hospital in Baghdad; Gutierrez, a 33-year-old social studies teacher from San Fernando High School in California, received negative reviews for teaching about Iraq and having students think critically about war; and Mayer, an elementary school teacher in Bloomington, Indiana, was fired after telling her students, "I honk for peace" on the eve of the Iraq war.)

Rather than continue to evade this crucial issue, it is time for teacher-educators, curriculum theorists, and social studies teachers to hold an open dialogue about how we teach the U.S. invasion and occupation of Iraq, as well as other American wars. For certain, these are issues of utmost importance. The war has been debated in Congress, covered in American newspapers, and featured on broadcast news programs. Yet NCSS has yet to foster an open discourse, a roundtable discussion, or craft a position statement on the war.

Whether it is in schools, political arenas, or in the media, raising questions about past and present American wars is a sensitive issue. For many Americans, supporting American wars and military operations is synonymous with patriotism and love for one's country. Longtime war correspondent Chris Hedges explains that "War as a myth begins with patriotism, which always begins with thinly veiled self-glorification. We exalt ourselves, our goodness, our decency, our humanity, and in that self-exaltation we denigrate the other" (Hedges, 2003, para. 6). Patriotic rhetoric and nationalism make it difficult, if not impossible, to talk freely about American motives, policies, and actions. Rather than critically examining American history, the mainstream media (which includes school textbook publishers) generally casts American foreign policy as a policy designed to defend democracy and free markets (Chomsky, 1989, p. 49). By failing to offer a critical analysis of American wars and military operations, citizens are treated as passive spectators whose duty it is to faithfully support U.S. policy.

Thus, the aim of this work is to initiate a discourse about how we teach about American wars. In examining textbook treatments of the Vietnam War, this work takes a critical approach. Critical theorists believe "knowledge is always an ideological construction linked to particular interests" (McLaren, 1998, p. 183). Whether we are constructing national standards, designing museum exhibits, or editing textbooks, we are working from "a system of values and beliefs which provide the concepts, images, and ideas by which people interpret their world and shape their behavior toward other people" (Bennett deMarrais & LeCompte, 1995, p. 319). Thus, our subjective positions are not ours alone, but are informed by dominant ideologies that are never neutral and always permeated "with interest, value, and judgment" (McLaren, 1998, p. 181). Or, as Paul Willis puts it, "Ideology is the 'them' in us" (Willis, 1977, p. 169). Institutions like schools and the mass media shape our understanding of who we are, where we should be going, and mediate our interactions with the outside world.

Whereas ideology influences the way in which we view the world, hegemony is a form of social control that is achieved in one of two ways. According to Gramsci, the first method is coercive power that relies on a police force and prison system to legally enforce discipline on those individuals or groups who do not consent to the status quo. The second method relies on "spontaneous consent" that is granted "by the great masses of the population to the general direction imposed on social life by the dominant fundamental group" (Gramsci, 1971/2005, p. 12). Whereby the first method relies on force, the second method is more insidious as

> the dominant culture tries to "fix" the meanings of signs, symbols, and representations to provide a common worldview, disguising relations of power and privilege through the organs of the mass media and state apparatus such as schools, government institutions, and state bureaucracies. (McLaren, 1998, p. 179)

As a critical theorist interested in the way schools can stifle critical thought and promote intellectual dependence, my intention is to uncover the overt and subtle ways that ideology shapes textbook treatments of the Vietnam War. In my effort to understand the way in which ideology influences historical narrative, this study traverses the fields of economics, history, sociology, political science, and cultural studies. Drawing from the social sciences, I explore textbook treatments of the Vietnam War as a means to investigate the larger question of "What function do high school history textbooks serve?" Rather than looking at the complete textbook narratives like Loewen has done in his best-selling book *Lies My Teacher Told Me* (1996), I have chosen to take an in-depth look at how textbooks depict the Vietnam War. This study directly compares textbook narratives to the leading scholarship and recent evidence. This approach illuminates the striking (and sometimes startling) differences between the textbook and the complex world of historical research, where conclusions are tentative, evidence is crucial, and history is continuously being questioned and rewritten.

This study is predicated on several assumptions about social studies instruction. The first assumption is that the instruction must assist students in developing the attitudes, skills, and intellect required to "see the written word as something other than truth incarnate" (Wood, 1998, p. 189). Students must be armed with the tools to identify political polemics and propaganda present in textbooks, cable and broadcast news, newspapers, internet blogs, and political speeches. The second assumption is that conventional forms of knowledge, or what Michael Apple (2000) calls "official knowledge," dominate the mass media, and serve to enculturate students into uncritically supporting conservative positions (for example, pro-military, pro-business). The third assumption is that teachers must assist students in developing a critical perspective and examining the wealth of information they encounter. Thus, powerful teaching provides students with the opportunity to examine ideology and offers methods, concepts, and evidence that challenge conventional, hegemonic views.

Historian Marilyn Young describes the Vietnam War as "a zone of contested meaning" because of the range of interpretations, perspectives, and conclusions about the meaning and lessons of America's military conflict (Young, 1991, p. 314). This is why I have intentionally selected the Vietnam War as a topic of investigation. Although the Vietnam War officially ended more than 3 decades ago, questions endure about the U.S. justification for war, what transpired in the Gulf of Tonkin in August 1964, the passage of the Gulf of Tonkin Resolution, and the media's influence on public opinion. For certain, the way we approach our study of the Vietnam War and the questions we ask influences the way that we understand the Iraq War and future U.S. military actions. These conclusions have as much to do with our study of the past as they do with our commitments to present policies and the future direction of American foreign policy.

Chapter 1 focuses on the political controversy associated with critically examining American wars. The first section examines the firestorm that surrounded the Smithsonian's Crossroads exhibit. This exhibit was designed to spark public discussion about the United States' use of atomic bombs on the largely civilian populations of Hiroshima and Nagasaki. I use this contentious event as a point of departure because it highlights how conservative forces mobilize and use political power to stifle challenges to a prevailing patriotic ideology that casts the United States as a land of opportunity and defender of democracy. This event is followed by an introduction to the concept of "public memory," and an overview of three perspectives of the Vietnam War. I close this chapter with a description of what military historian Andrew Bacevich (2005) describes as the "New American Militarism."

The second chapter walks the reader through the textbook production process. It is estimated that four multinational publishing houses produce 80% of high school social studies textbooks (American Textbook Council, 2006). This raises questions about whether teachers and students have access to a range of high-quality textbooks that reflect the leading historical scholarship and provide opportunities for critical thought. In my investigation of the textbook production process, I examine the business aspect of textbook publishing, the divided market of open and closed adoption states, and the way in which textbook companies budget their resources. This is followed by a detailed description of how textbooks are written, the peculiar role of the author, and the political forces that influence the final narrative. I close Chapter 2 by highlighting the problems created by large corporations whose primary aim it is to get books adopted in key states, ensuring favorable returns on multimillion dollar investments.

Chapters 3 and 4 explore textbook treatments of two critical events: the Gulf of Tonkin Crisis of 1964 and the Tet Offensive of 1968. Historians consider these events to be major turning points in the Vietnam War. With President Johnson's public announcement of American reprisals for alleged attacks on American ships, the Gulf of Tonkin Crisis marked our official entry into the war. The Tet Offensive is also considered to be a critical event that clearly demonstrated that the United States' war effort was failing. Although public support was waning prior to 1968, the winter offensive contradicted the Johnson Administration's claims of American progress and forced a series of talks about a negotiated settlement. Textbook treatments of these two events are compared with leading histories and the most recent findings. In making comparisons, I have taken a close look at the scope of textbook narratives, the evidence presented, how controversy is handled, and the perspective from which the story is told.

The final chapter explores the ways in which classroom teachers can move beyond transmitting historical myth and provide students with authentic intellectual encounters with the historical record. By embracing the complexity of war, this chapter offers a heuristic predicated on six concepts: (1) war-making is a human construction, not an inevitable force; (2) international law provides a framework from which students can examine the rationale for and execution of military conflict; (3) the media plays an important role in building consensus for war; (4) attending to voices of opposition is essential to understanding war; (5) political language is used to build consensus for war; and (6) deconstructing textbook narratives is a powerful way to examine the myth of war.

Finally, my aim is not to condemn publishing companies, textbook authors, the U.S. military, public officials, or social studies teachers. Senator J. William Fulbright, a key figure in the Vietnam War, explains, "To criticize one's country is to do it a service and pay it a compliment. It is a service because it may spur the country to do better than it is doing. It is a compliment because it evidences a belief that the country can do better than it is doing" (Fulbright, 1966, p. 25). This study is written out of a deep respect for creative and talented public educators and a desire to see social studies theorists and practitioners engage in a discussion about the relationship between war-making and history education. It is my belief that this discussion is long overdue. At this particular time in American history, the Obama administration has failed to articulate a coherent strategy for winning the peace or altogether ending the wars in Afghanistan and Iraq, the global economy is on the brink of ruin, defense spending has reached unsustainable levels, private corporations are actively involved in shaping education policy, and the U.S. military is making unprecedented demands on American schools. A robust discussion about our profession and our place in these troublesome times is absolutely vital. If we are serious about preparing our students for democratic citizenship, we can settle for nothing less.

CHAPTER 1

The Atomic Bomb, the Vietnam War, and the New American Militarism

.

In January 1995, the Smithsonian National Museum of Air and Space planned an exhibit commemorating the 50th anniversary of the end of World War II. Based on 30 years of research and 8 years of planning, the museum designed the five-room exhibit entitled "Crossroads: The End of World War II, the Atomic Bomb, and the Origins of the Cold War," to stimulate public discussion about the first use of nuclear weapons. Historian Richard Kohn, who served as chairman of the Smithsonian's Research and Collections Management Advisory Committee, explained that the exhibition's "primary goal was to encourage visitors to make a thoughtful and balanced reexamination of the atomic bombings in the light of the political and military factors leading to the decision to use the bomb, the human suffering experienced by the people of Hiroshima and Nagasaki, and the long-term implications of the events of August 6 and 9, 1945" (Kohn, 1995, p. 1041). Tom Engelhardt, writing for *Harper's Magazine*, described the exhibit as linking the unlinkable:

the burnished plane with the human suffering it caused and continues to cause; smiling shots of boisterous young airmen with unbearable images of seared victims; the consciousness of those who fought in World War II with the consciousness of those who grew up in the penumbra of World War III; the celebratory with the crematory; the just with the unjust; victory with defeat. (Engelhardt, 1996, p. 172)

The exhibit's original design offered patrons five sections chronicling the overall brutality of the Pacific War, the decision to drop the bomb, the development of the B-29, and the training of the 509th Composite Group that piloted the *Enola Gay*, the destruction and human suffering wrought by the bomb, as well as Japan's surrender and the beginning of the Cold War (Nobile, 1995). The first room included an oversized photograph of the aircraft carrier *Bunker Hill*, inflamed after two kamikaze attacks. Drawing attention to the development of the atom bomb, the second room featured passages from President Truman's and Secretary of State Henry Stimson's diaries and an original copy of Albert Einstein's letter to President Franklin D. Roosevelt warning that Germany had the capacity to build an atomic bomb. The third room presented the *Enola Gay*'s fully restored 56-foot fuselage discharging a replica uranium bomb. This room was given "a human touch" by featuring photographs, letters, and other artifacts sent in by the members of the 509th Composite group. Along with photographs of Japanese civilians burned by the bomb, the fourth room was designed to be "a deliberately passionate text" as it included a child's charred lunchbox, scorched clothing, a wooden clog, and a watch with its hands frozen at the precise moment of the bombing. The final section of the exhibit featured a small theater where museum patrons could view a 15-minute film featuring the crews of the *Enola Gay* and *Bockscar* voicing their feelings about the bombing 50 years later (Harwit, 1995, pp. 1068–1074).

None of the National Museum of Air and Space's 8 million annual visitors saw the exhibit as it was originally designed. World War II veterans felt that the questions posed by the *Enola Gay* exhibit did not reflect the American mindset during World War II or the context of the bombing of Hiroshima and Nagasaki. Veterans were especially concerned that the exhibit discounted the number of lives the atomic bomb "saved" by bringing an immediate end to the war, failed to represent veterans' viewpoints, judged the morality of the bombing from a perspective 50 years removed, and implicitly criticized the effectiveness of strategic bombing (Harwit, 1996, pp. 126–149). Past and present leaders of the military community also criticized the exhibit for being unpatriotic. John Correll, Editor in Chief of the Air Force Association's (AFA) *Air Force Magazine,* described the exhibit as portraying "the Japanese as desperate defenders of homeland and culture, the Americans as ruthless invaders, driven by racism and revenge" (Correll, 1994, p. 2). Brigadier General Paul Tibbets, commander of the 509th composite Group, denounced the exhibit as "a package of insults" for failing to present the use of atomic bombs within the "context of the times" (Engelhardt, 1996, p. 73). On January 19th, William Detweiler, National Commander of the American Legion, sent President Clinton a letter calling for "the immediate resignation and termination of the Director of the National Air and Space Museum" along with a "fresh and unbiased . . . balanced exhibit" (Detweiler, 1995, as cited in Harwit, 1995, p. 1081).

The Crossroads exhibit also drew fire from Congressional leaders from both sides of the aisle. Senator Diane Feinstein (D) of California questioned whether the Smithsonian's curators had the right to "interpret history rather than just simply to put forward historical facts based on the validity of the fact and the historical value" (as cited in Prosise, 1998, p. 328). GOP House leader Newt Gingrich complained that the Crossroads exhibit was tainted by "a certain political correctness seeping in and distorting and prejudicing the Smithsonian's exhibits." He went on to argue that "Political correctness may be O.K. in some faculty lounge, but the Smithsonian is a treasure that belongs to the American people and it should not become a plaything for left-wing ideologies" (as cited in Goldberger, 1996, p. 2.26). The *Wall Street Journal* echoed Gingrich's sentiments by charging that the Smithsonian Museum of Air and Space "was now in the hands of academics unable to view American history as anything other than a woeful catalogue of crimes and aggressions against helpless people of the Earth" (War and the Smithsonian, 1994, p. A10).

Under intense criticism from the military community and facing the Republican Congress's threat of withdrawing public funds, Smithsonian Secretary Michael Heyman canceled the exhibit. The public would not see the powerful images of the Pacific War, the development of the nuclear bombs, and the destruction and human suffering they produced. Instead of offering the public a rich, provocative exhibit designed to spark a public discussion about the lessons to be drawn from the bombings of Hiroshima and Nagasaki, the Crossroads exhibit was reduced to a safe, sanitary display of American military might. Conservative forces prevailed as the National Museum of Air and Space replaced the Crossroads exhibit with a four-room exhibit featuring the fuselage and other parts of the *Enola Gay,* cheerful accounts from the plane's restorers, a video of the *Enola Gay's* crew, and flight statistics on the B-29. Banished from the National Museum of Air and Space were the larger questions surrounding Truman's rationale for dropping the bombs, the effectiveness of the strategic bombing campaign, and the morality of bombing civilian population centers. In the end, the Smithsonian offered the American public a censored, sterilized exhibit of one of the most destructive events in human history.

HISTORICAL MEMORY AND THE SELECTIVE TRADITION

The debate about the Crossroads exhibit is a shining example of how political forces, both liberal and conservative, can be parlayed to preserve and promote a public memory that casts the United States as a benevolent superpower intent on spreading democracy, honoring international law, and preserving peace and order. Bodnar (1992) explains that public memory is chiefly concerned with "fundamental issues about the entire existence of a society: its organization, structure of power, and the very meaning of the past and present" (Bodnar, 1992, p. 14). Rather than a provocative exhibit designed to foster an open dialogue about the use of atomic weapons against a largely civilian population, military leaders and conservative pundits, both Democrats and Republicans, ensured that the final exhibit celebrated military technology instead. All societies have a tendency to manage the reconstruction of the past to be compatible with the needs and purposes of the present. This process is led by political and economic elites who use schools, the mass media, and popular culture as instruments to faithfully transmit a particular tradition, set of values, beliefs, or customs from one generation to the next. By coloring the way we interpret the past, these traditions shape our national identity and establish parameters for normative discourse and political action. This is what is widely known as the "selective tradition" (Williams, 1961). The result of this selective process is that alternative interpretations are often lost or suppressed so that the past can be seen in ways that are compatible with dominant values and ideologies.

The selective tradition has a tremendous influence on what is taught in the classroom. A variety of institutional mechanisms ensure that history is taught in ways that support the status quo and socialize students into accepting the dominant political, economic, and social realities. State curriculum guides, standardized tests, and corporate textbooks not only regulate what is and is not taught, but also the perspective from which history is taught, the pace of instruction, instructional methods, and, ultimately, determine what counts as historical knowledge. This book examines the ways in which the selective tradition shapes how military conflict is presented in textbooks. Apple (2000) explains that textbooks "participate in creating what a society has recognized as legitimate and truthful. They help set the canons of truthfulness and, as such, also help recreate a major reference point for what knowledge, culture, belief, and morality really are" (p. 46). Textbooks and curricula materials draw upon war as a major frame of reference, marking progress toward an abstract, and perhaps unrealizable, democratic ideal. Traditional history treats the U.S. war on Native Americans, the Revolutionary, Civil, and World Wars, as a series of triumphs, each bringing the nation one step closer to greatness. Faithfully attending the heroic deeds of military greats like Custer, Washington, Lee, Eisenhower, and MacArthur, textbooks transmit the myth that redemptive violence is a legitimate, even appealing, solution to international and domestic problems. Lost from textbook narratives and curricular objectives are the demands that war makes on our democratic institutions, its costs in both blood and treasure, and the myriad stories of Americans who struggled to limit war through nonviolent alternatives (Juhnke & Hunter, 2001).

The Struggle for National Standards

To fully appreciate the dynamics of the selective tradition, it is necessary to acknowledge the myriad ways tradition is both contested and preserved. Michael Kammen explains that efforts to challenge established tradition are met by calls for reconciliation, uniting the citizenry, and strengthening our common bonds (Kammen, 1991). This is exactly what happened in 1994, when high school history teachers, school administrators, curriculum supervisors, parents, librarians, curriculum specialists, and historians representing 33 professional organizations convened on the campus of UCLA at the National Center for History at Schools (NCHS) to develop voluntary national standards for history education. In its original form, *The National Standards for United States History* was a 245-page teaching guide comprised of teaching resources, examples of student achievement, 31 standards, and 395 elaborated standards representing 10 eras of U.S. history. Charlotte Crabtree (a UCLA professor of curricular studies and founding director of the National Center for History in Schools) and Gary Nash (a UCLA professor of history and the author of *The American Odyssey*, one of the textbooks investigated in this study) designed the standards "to go beyond the facts presented in their textbooks and to examine the historical record for themselves" (NCHS, 1994, p. 17). These new standards were unique in that they did not represent a monolithic American past told from a single perspective. Drawing upon labor history and the experiences of women, African Americans, Native Americans, and a number of immigrant groups, the new standards required teachers and students to actively explore American history through a host of perspectives and by using a variety of inquiry-based activities.

Even before the *National Standards for United States History* were available to the public, Lynne Cheney wrote an editorial for the *Wall Street Journal* entitled "The End of History" (Cheney, 1994). In it, Cheney sharply criticized the national standards for failing to pay homage to traditional heroes like Thomas Edison, Robert E. Lee, J.P. Morgan, Paul Revere, George Washington, and the Wright Brothers. She also criticized the history standards for what she considered an unwarranted emphasis on the American Federation of Labor, the Ku Klux Klan, Joseph McCarthy, the National Organization of Women, and Harriet Tubman. Conservative educator Diane Ravitch and conservative columnists Charles Krauthammer and John Leo publicly denounced the project for representing a left-wing slant and failing a traditional approach to history that emphasizes facts, dates, and events. Rush Limbaugh took up Cheney's cause by telling his listeners that the *National Standards* (which he described as a "bastardization of history") should be flushed "down the sewer of multiculturalism" (as cited in Nash, Crabtree, & Dunn, 1997, p. 5).

The standards controversy came to a head immediately after the Republican Party won control of Congress by gaining 54 seats in the House of Representatives and 8 seats in the Senate in the midterm elections of 1994. On January 18, 1995, the Senate voted 99-1 (Democratic Senator Bennett Johnson of Louisiana was the only dissenting vote) to officially censure the history standards and withdraw federal funds from the project. In place of the original history standards the Senate resolution called for a new set of standards that emphasized the United States contributions to global freedom and prosperity (Cohen, 1996).

After intense public debate, and faced with losing federal funding, Nash and Crabtree agreed to form an independent panel of "unassailable, fair-minded, and knowledgeable persons" to review the standards, defuse the controversy, and write a second set of history standards that conservative critics and congressional leaders would find acceptable (Nash, Crabtree, & Dunn, 1997, p. 245). In the summer of 1995, this panel, led by Christopher Cross, president of the Council for Basic Education, reviewed the standards and suggested they be revised by expanding treatment of particular subjects and eliminating biased language. The result was a much more celebratory body of standards that glossed over differences of race and class. For instance, in the original version, Era 9, standard 3C required high school students to demonstrate their understanding of the Vietnam war by "analyzing growing disillusionment with the war" (7–12), "analyzing the impact of class and race on wartime mobilization" (9–12), and "analyzing the Kennedy, Johnson, and Nixon Administrations' Vietnam policy and the consequences of the escalation of the war" (NCHS, 1994, p. 218). The panel elected for a much more patriotic treatment of the war by eliminating any references to race, class, the draft, or public disillusionment (NCHS, 1996, p. 124). In the end, educators and historians representing 33 national organizations accepted the revisions to appease powerful conservative critics who mobilized to preserve the selective tradition.

The Dangers of Doing History

The standards controversy exemplifies one episode of a larger conservative campaign to control the social studies curriculum and the way the past is presented in the public schools. The Thomas B. Fordham Foundation, a conservative think tank based in New York City, has published a series of reports criticizing progressive teaching methods, multicultural education, critical inquiry, cooperative learning, and global education.

Recently, the Fordham Foundation has also sought to build consensus about the legitimacy of the American war in Iraq and consensus for the Bush administration's policy of preventive war. In response to the U.S. invasion of Iraq, the Fordham Foundation published a manual entitled "Terrorists, Despots, and Democracy: What Our Children Need to Know" (TDD). This report criticizes education leaders Michael Apple and Alfie Kohn and organizations such the National Education Association, the Muslim Education Council, the American Red Cross, and the National Council for Social Studies for being unpatriotic. Calling on educators to blindly support the wars in Afghanistan and Iraq, a cadre of conservative educational activists including Chester Finn Jr., William Bennett, Lynne Cheney, Victor Davis Hanson, E. D. Hirsch Jr., and Lamar Alexander argue that students should be taught that 9/11 was an attack on American values, that Islamic fundamentalism is the cause of terrorism, and that the wars in Iraq and Afghanistan are supported by Just War theory. The Fordham Foundation's TDD steers teachers and students away from a critical examination of American foreign policy, the United States history of military excursions into the Middle East, Iraq's vast oil resources, and the Geneva Conventions. In a bald defense of U.S. preemptive strikes against Iraq, Conservative historian Victor Davis Hanson reminds teachers that "Failing to exercise moral judgment—denying Islamic fundamentalism and fascism is a great plague on the world that would destroy the rights of women, the very notion of religious tolerance, and all the gifts of the Enlightenment, is not proof of forbearance but of abject ethical aptitude" (Hanson, 2003, p. 23).

The Fordham Foundation's efforts to manage the way we teach about 9/11 and the wars in Afghanistan and Iraq, is one part of larger conservative alliance of ideologues, right-wing scholars, and conservative foundations that view schools as sites to promote patriotism, instill reverence for traditional values and worldviews, and transmit a common core curriculum (Bennett, 1998, p. 38; Hirsch, 1996; Ravitch, 2003). This campaign rests on several assumptions about teachers, learning, and assessment:

- Lacking the ability to make sense of the complex world, teachers and students need outside experts and political elites to guide them in crafting curricula, defining what is and is not acceptable content, and what counts as legitimate historical knowledge
- History teaching is an act of political socialization fixing parameters on what is considered acceptable content and activity, and ensuring students are offered a hegemonic interpretation of past events
- The social studies curriculum is conceptualized as a static outline of people, events, and concepts that reinforces consensus values and mainstream historical interpretations, effectively preparing students for accepting the status quo
- Testing mechanisms are essential instruments that monitor classroom instruction and measure the degree to which students accept, internalize, and recite the formal curriculum

Approaching history education in this fashion suggests a false sense of consensus and robs students of exploring the myriad ways in which the past can be viewed. Cleansing the historical record of unwanted events, perspectives, and voices, and attending to positive aspects of American history and life transforms the past into myth. Historical myth simplifies the past, imbues events with meaning they do not have, and functions to stifle critical thought. For example, only by ignoring voices of opposition, downplaying economic motivations, and cutting away from civilian death and ecological destruction can American foreign policy be rendered a policy designed to defend democracy and free markets. Likewise, only by calling our attention to success stories and downplaying institutionalized racism, class, and gender inequities, can we create the myth that the U.S. economic system is a meritocracy where those who play by the rules and work hard can get ahead and achieve the American dream. When these distorted historical memories are endorsed by teachers and transmitted to children via the textbook, curricula, and classroom instruction, historical memory becomes historical myth and teaching becomes an act of political socialization.

Whereas traditional approaches to history education accept historical myth without qualification, a critical approach actively examines the way in which myth is produced, distributed, and related to political power. Teachers concerned with providing students authentic intellectual encounters with the past must ask whose interests are being served by the textbook, methods, and curricula we use to reconstruct the past. As public school teachers charged with preparing students for active citizenship, we must not only examine our practices, but we must also seek out alternative practices, evidence, and perspectives that may lead to a more complete understanding of the past. For instance, by questioning Truman's decision to drop the bomb and including the perspectives of American military and political leaders as well as those of Japanese civilians, Michael Harwit and the Smithsonian staff challenged Americans to evaluate evidence and think critically about U.S. foreign policy, the unfettered use of military power, and civilian suffering. By including artifacts that put a human face on the massive civilian suffering, it was designed to encourage visitors to consider the moral dimensions of industrial warfare. Rather than treating U.S. military action as something to be accepted and even celebrated, the Crossroads exhibit invited the public to examine and evaluate the historical record for themselves.

This study explores how the selective tradition shapes the way the Vietnam War is presented textbooks. I have chosen textbooks as objects of analysis as they are the centerpiece of social studies instruction. Studies have shown that textbooks serve as the primary resource for teaching American and World history (U.S. Department of Education, 2001, pp. 33, 109, 111). Teachers draw upon the all-encompassing narratives to meet the hundreds of required topics found in the American history and World history curricula. Nonetheless, textbooks reflect the selective tradition as corporate publishers make decisions about perspective, voice, evidence, and organization. The perspective from which the narrative is told, the content that is included and excluded, and the evidence employed to support the narrative direct students' attention to what is considered "legitimate" knowledge. Indeed, several analyses have found that textbook narratives tell the story of American progress by placing the European American experience and achievements at the center of history while marginalizing minority groups, women, and people with disabilities (Fitzgerald, 1979; Sleeter & Grant, 1991; U.S. Commission on Civil Rights, 1980). After repeated exposure to such textbooks through years of schooling, as well as other sources of hegemony (e.g., television, commercial advertising, popular music), traditional values, perspectives, and experiences become social reality. "This reality," Michael Apple explains, "saturates our very consciousness, so that the educational, economic, and social world we see and interact with . . . becomes the world *tout court,* the only world" (Apple, 1979, p. 5).

THE VIETNAM WAR: "A ZONE OF CONTESTED MEANING"

Acknowledging the political nature of remembering war, this study examines how textbooks treat another controversial chapter of American history that resists simplification, the Vietnam War. Like the bombings of Hiroshima and Nagasaki, the Vietnam War is another historical chapter mired in controversy and intense political debate. Spanning 25 years (1950–1975), the Vietnam War is the longest war in American history. It cost the United States $167 billion and resulted in the death of 58,000 American soldiers and an estimated 2–3 million Vietnamese, Cambodians, and Laotians (Herring, 1991, p. 113). Soldiers, officers, and historians disagree about U.S. justification for escalation, the wisdom of military strategy and battlefield tactics, the moral dimension of aerial bombing and the application of chemical herbicides, and the myriad causes for U.S. failure (Herring, 1987).

    I have intentionally selected the Vietnam War because it resists simplification and provides a series of narratives that contradict the basic tenets of the myth of war. Daniel Ellsberg's leaking of *The Penta-*

gon Papers provides a documentary record of illegal U.S. activities that include covert raids against North Vietnam, the Kennedy administration's involvement in assassinating South Vietnamese President Ngo Din Diem, and the U.S. bombing of Laos and Cambodia. A vigorous, well-organized antiwar movement comprised of religious activists, leftists, women's groups, public intellectuals, and college students also complicates the narrative by calling attention to the myriad reasons for opposing the war. The violent suppression of the antiwar protests at the Pentagon, Chicago, and Kent State also raise questions about the relationship between free speech and state power. The Vietnam Veterans Against the War further complicates the narrative by calling attention to American soldiers' disenchantment with the war and damaging testimony about U.S. conduct and American atrocities.

For many Americans it has come to represent an archetype for a misguided costly U.S. military intervention that exposes the limits of U.S. military power and the folly of fighting a protracted war thousands of miles from home without a formal declaration or the full support of the citizenry. Bruce Nelan, writing for *Time* magazine 20 years after the U.S. withdrawal from Vietnam, described Vietnam as a "lost war" that many Americans believed was fought for the false assumption that China was intent on dominating Southeast Asia, creating the illusion that Vietnam was a critical battleground in the Cold War (Nelan, 1995, p. 45). Political conservatives, however, see this critical interpretation, referred to as the Vietnam syndrome (a term coined by the Reagan administration), as a psychological restraint responsible for the American public's refusal to unequivocally support Cold War military spending and interventions to secure and promote U.S. global interests (Lefever, 1997).

Rather than avoiding discord and disagreement, teachers can seize upon the Vietnam War as an opportunity to learn about how evidence, interpretation, perspective, and human hands shape historical narrative. In this next section I highlight three major perspectives on the Vietnam War: the orthodox, revisionist, and critical (Hess, 1994). These three perspectives demonstrate the subjective nature of historical study and the ways in which authors' idiosyncratic values and political sensibilities influence how they interpret the historical record and write about the past. This is not intended to be a comprehensive review of the histories of the Vietnam War; rather, its purpose is to provide the reader with a general sense of the complex nature of writing history as well as the contentious issues that shape our understanding of the Vietnam War.

The Orthodox Perspective

At the heart of the orthodox perspective is the quagmire thesis. The quagmire thesis holds that the United States, blinded by illusions of American military omnipotence and paranoid about a global social-ist movement orchestrated from Moscow, initiated a war in Vietnam that it could not win. The orthodox view underscores the notion that containment policy, originally articulated by George Kennan as a way to check Soviet expansion, was inappropriately applied to Vietnam. Failing to appreciate the political dynamics of Vietnam and its long struggle for independence, key members of the Kennedy and Johnson administrations crafted inappropriate policies that fueled the resis-tance, placed the American government on the wrong side of an inde-pendence movement, and committed American men and resources to fighting a hopeless battle in an unfamiliar land (Cooper, 1970; Draper, 1967; Halberstam, 1969). Not only did these policies lead to failure, General Westmoreland's call for high body counts often led to un-necessary civilian deaths and in some instances atrocities, which in turn led to increasing opposition to U.S. troops and badly damaged American prestige (Gibson, 1986). George Herring, a leading Vietnam scholar, sums up the orthodox position this way:

> By intervening in what was essentially a local struggle, it placed itself at the mercy of local forces, a weak client, and a determined adversary. What might have remained a local conflict with primarily local impli-cations turned into a major international conflict with enormous hu-man costs. (2002b, pp. 357–358)

The Revisionist Perspective

For revisionists, the lessons to be learned are quite different. While lamenting American losses, the revisionist perspective suggests that the war was a noble effort fought to check communist expansion, but mishandled by civilian and military policymakers, and subverted by the American antiwar movement. Conservative writers indict Presi-dent Lyndon Johnson and Secretary of Defense Robert McNamara for failing to properly plan and execute the war.

It was not the jungle terrain, nor the communists' determination, but the policy of gradual escalation that resulted in a prolonged, inef-fectual war strategy that cost $150 billion and the loss of 58,000 U.S. soldiers (Palmer, 1978; Sharp, 1979; Summers, 1984). Failed policies, poor leadership, and critical media reports all combined to fuel the antiwar movement and force Nixon to withdraw American political, fiscal, and military support, prematurely ending the Vietnam War at a time when American forces, under General Creighton Abrams leadership, were making progress in both urban centers and the countryside (Sorley, 1999).

These revisionist histories insist that the United States not be discouraged by its failures and recoil into an era of isolationism, but must learn from Vietnam and be better prepared for future wars. Rather than place limits or adopt a cautious foreign policy, revisionists contend that there will be more "Vietnams" in the future and that "the United States should improve its capabilities to engage in unconventional, low-intensity conflict in wars, including civil wars, in cases where the outcome is important for American global strategy" (Lind, 1999, p. 277).

The Critical Perspective

Whereas the orthodox and revisionist perspectives center on American policies and leaders, and disagree about whether or not American intervention was justified, the critical perspective asks larger questions about American motives and conduct. Historians Gabriel Kolko, Howard Zinn, and Marilyn Young depict the Vietnam War as a military adventure to extend U.S. hegemony to Southeast Asia. Kolko, who describes himself as a radical scholar, argues that in the post-war period,

> The United States was the major inheritor of the mantle of imperialism in modern history, acting not out of a desire to defend the nation against some tangible threat to its physical welfare but because it sought to create a controllable, responsible order elsewhere, one that would permit the political destinies of distant places to evolve in a manner beneficial to American goals far surpassing the immediate needs of its domestic society. (1985, p. 73)

Critical historians contend that the United States, primarily concerned with promoting American interests and projecting U.S. power, chose to wage an immoral war in which civilian abuses and widespread atrocities were common. Young (1991) chronicles how the United States committed a number unspeakable acts, ranging from the installation of Ngo Din Diem, who tortured and executed his political opponents, to the widespread application of hundreds of millions of pounds of herbicides on over 4 million acres of South Vietnam between 1962 and 1970 (Young, 1991, p. 82). In one of the earliest critical studies of the Vietnam War, Zinn (1967) highlights U.S. support of dictatorships throughout Central and South America, Africa, the Middle East, and Asia and argues that the war in Vietnam must be viewed as a continuation of the same foreign policy. He explains that the nature of the Vietnam War, with its tactical use of high altitude bombing, artillery fire, and search and destroy missions, resulted in mass civilian deaths. Zinn describes 26 separate U.S. atrocities and contends that this "is only a tiny known part of an enormous pattern of devastation which, if seen in its entirety, would have to be described as one of the most evil acts committed by any nation in modern times" (p. 59).

These three historical perspectives on the Vietnam War highlight the dynamic nature of historical study and the multiple ways of interpreting the past. It is exactly what one might expect in a democratic society where the free flow of information is considered a vital part of public life. Perhaps more importantly, the disagreement about the nature and meaning of the Vietnam War highlights the significance of remembering war, the role it has (and continues to) play in American life, and the lessons we can draw upon in examining our present foreign policy and military operations.

THE EMERGING U.S. MILITARISM AND AMERICAN SCHOOLS

At the time of this writing the United States is engaged in wars in Afghanistan and Iraq, key provisions of the Patriot Act have been extended, military spending has reached an all-time high, the national debt has surpassed 10 trillion dollars, and the American economy is weakening. A growing number of scholars, both liberal and conservative (Bacevich, 2006; Boggs, 2005; Johnson, 2004), interpret these trends as a sign of a new era of American militarism and endless war. By militarism I mean the "phenomenon by which a nation's armed services come to put their institutional preservation ahead of achieving national security or even a commitment to the integrity of the governmental structure of which they are a part of" (Johnson, 2004, pp. 23–24).

Military historian Andrew Bacevich (2006) argues that the United States has entered a dangerous new era of American militarism where preventive war has replaced the various forms of containment policy drawn upon by the Truman, Eisenhower, Kennedy, Johnson, Nixon, Carter, Reagan, Bush Sr., and Clinton administrations. This new aggressive foreign policy substitutes unilateral military operations for traditional diplomacy and multilateral operations. This go-it-alone approach is responsible for unprecedented levels of military spending. The United States' annual military budget has increased from approximately $333 billion dollars in 2001 to $700 billion in 2007. The military budget is used to finance a sprawling network of 725 military bases abroad and another 969 located within the United States (Laxler, 2007, p. 112). The United States presently leads the world in military spending, with 45% of the world total, followed by the United Kingdom, China, France, and Japan, with 4–5% each (Stockholm International Peace Research Institute, 2008, para. 3). It is estimated that in 2008 the United States will devote more money to military spending than Europe, China, the Middle East, Russia, and Latin America combined (GlobalIssues.org, 2008).

American militarism reaches far beyond foreign policy initiatives, the Pentagon, and its military bases. It is an integral part of the American economy. Building the instruments of war is one of the last viable manufacturing sectors of the faltering American economy, where an era of globalization and free trade agreements has resulted in massive outsourcing of production jobs. The largest U.S. defense contractor is Lockheed Martin. In 2008 it had a net sales of $42.7 billion with a backlog of $80.9 billion in unfilled contracts. It employs 140,000 people and has 1,000 facilities in 500 cities and 46 U.S. states (Lockheed Martin, 2009).

Lockheed Martin represents one leg of what is known as the Iron Triangle of interest groups that comprise the Military Industrial Complex. The military leadership at the Pentagon and congressional defense committees represent the other two. The way it works is simple. Members of Congress compete for military contracts for complex multimillion dollar projects like the F-22 fighter jet (which has yet to be used in Iraq or Afghanistan) that provide jobs in several states. The Pentagon decides which projects are worth funding and which are not. The projects that get funded channel money toward one region and away from others. When defense spending increases the Pentagon gets new military hardware; members of Congress get credit for creating economic opportunities; plant workers, engineers, and executives are guaranteed work; and Lockheed Martin shareholders enjoy increases in earnings. Cuts in military spending, however, can mean factory closures; layoffs for machinists, managers, and engineers; and in extreme cases, the collapse of entire communities (Greider, 1998). The best way to ensure the economic fortunes of Lockheed Martin employees and the communities in which they reside is to continuously allocate more and more American tax dollars to the production of military armaments.

While military spending is essential to sustain the American economy, military organizations are deeply involved in shaping civilian life as well. RAND (Research and Development) is a civilian corporation paid by the U.S. government to conduct scientific research on how to wage and win wars effectively. Founded by Air Force general Henry Arnold to maintain U.S. military superiority in the post–World War II period, RAND researchers (which include a number of Nobel Prize winners) are responsible for crafting U.S. military strategy in Vietnam, the Cold War, and most recently Iraq. RAND is well-known for developing Rational Choice Theory, which posits that all human behavior is motivated by self-interest. Whether it be military conflict or welfare programs, this theory assumes that people generally look out for their self-interest first and the common good is only a secondary consideration. This theory shapes the way Americans think about finance, trade, taxation, and social policy (Abella, 2008). RAND analysts are currently working closely with the federal government on a variety of education policy issues that include assessment, school choice, and merit pay, policies for which the Obama administration has expressed support.

The new American militarism can also be observed in American culture. Former military leaders Norman Schwarzkopf, Wesley Clarke, and Colin Powell are lionized in the media and actively involved in the Republican and Democratic parties. Top-selling video games like *Medal of Honor, Call of Duty,* and *Ghost Recon* dehumanize American enemies, distort the combat experience, and introduce American youth to military culture (Bacevich, 2006). Capitalizing on teens' preoccupation with video games and virtual worlds, the Pentagon has devised an online interactive military simulation entitled America's Army. Launched on July 4, 2002, this online combat simulator is a recruitment tool that allows teens to "take a virtual test drive of the U.S. military." It allows teens to choose combat roles, select weapons, and complete individual and collective training missions to earn Green Beret status. At the time of this writing, 10 million people are registered players on America's Army (America's Army, 2009).

Sustaining the new American militarism requires the Pentagon to become increasingly involved in the nation's public schools and colleges. In the last 2 decades, a de facto partnership has been forged between the Department of Education (DOE) and Department of Defense (DOD). This marriage has produced a variety of federal mandates and programs that guarantee the U.S. military unprecedented access to public schools. In 1994, the DOE and DOD created the Troops-to-Teachers (TTT) program. TTT, which has offices in 31 states, assists military personnel who have served for 6 years in meeting certification requirements and acquiring public school teaching positions in low-income communities (Troops to Teachers, 2008, para. 3). Military personnel who complete 3-year stints in schools where 50% of the students are eligible for free and reduced lunch programs are awarded stipends of up to $10,000. This program, while billed as a necessary measure to meet teacher shortages in impoverished urban and rural areas, all but guarantees that teachers with pro-military values and ties to recruiters will be serving the nation's poorest students, many of whom will lack the skills to attend college or compete in the shrinking job market.

Federal legislation also ensures military access to more affluent school districts and the nation's colleges and universities. The Solomon Amendment, enacted in 1996, authorizes the Secretary of Defense to determine any college or university ineligible for federal contracts and grants for preventing military recruiters access to campus, the student body, or student directory information. Similarly, the No Child Left Behind Act requires every federally funded school district to provide the U.S. military with the students' names, addresses, and phone numbers. The Pentagon currently maintains a massive database of personal information and areas of study for approximately 30 million 16- to 25-year-olds (Leave My Child Alone, 2009).

In addition to placing teachers in classrooms and storing personal information, the U.S. Army has devised a "School Recruiting Operations handbook." The *Recruiting Operations* Handbook (2006) organizes recruiting around the principles of war where maneuvers are guided by economy of force, unity of command, simplicity, and surprise. Employing the principles of war, the recruiting handbook depicts civilian communities as potential recruiting "targets," schools as "battlefields," and high school students as "the enemy" (Agostinone-Wilson, 2008, p. 5; U.S. Army Recruiting Command, 2006, pp. 1–6 & 1–7). Military recruiters analyze socioeconomic indicators that include unemployment rates, housing data (e.g., owning versus renting), lifestyle choices (e.g., purchasing habits, work patterns, and attitudes), and psychographics (e.g., a population's wants, needs, and desires) to determine the appropriate recruiting strategy. Once a community is defined and a strategy is formulated, recruiters take the offensive:

> Taking the offensive means that decisive recruiting operations, such as lead generation and prospecting, continue virtually nonstop. Recruiters become a living presence in their communities, and ask everyone they meet for referrals. Recruiters continually expand their network of influencers, and they tell the Army story at every opportunity. Recruiters

and their leaders become role models for young people and lead them
to fulfillment through service to country. (U.S. Army Recruiting Command, 2006, pp. 1–6)

These new recruiting tactics can be observed in high schools across the
United States. In suburban and working-class schools military recruiters have become a part of the school culture, leading drills at football
practice, sponsoring homecoming events, and even providing teachers with coffee and doughnuts (Herbert, 2005). In its efforts to meet
recruitment quotas, New Jersey's National Guard has provided teachers and students with opportunities to ride in Blackhawk helicopters,
fire mock assault rifles, and drive humvees (Asbury Park Press, 2006,
online).

In inner cities like Chicago, the U.S. military actually runs several schools. Brian Roa, who teaches science at Chicago's Senn High
School (which houses both a public school and a military academy),
describes how Rickover Naval Academy (RNA), one of several military
academies in Chicago Public School system, has created a two-tiered
system of schooling under the same roof. As a larger part of the priva-
tization of Chicago's public schools, RNA was initially promoted as a
school choice option, where ex-service personnel teach "cadets" both
a college prep curriculum and a military curriculum. Forced to choose
between sending their children to an underfunded public school or
the fully-funded RNA (which is sponsored by the Department of Defense) with better facilities, many parents choose RNA (Roa, 2009).

The United States' shift toward militarism, the ongoing struggles
to regulate the social studies curriculum, and the political parameters
placed on how we remember past wars underscore the importance
of engaging the past as a resource for understanding and addressing
our present problems. At this critical time, it is absolutely essential to
equip our students with the knowledge and skills to face these challenges. We may no longer have the luxury of choosing not to engage these issues. As defense budgets rise, resources will be diverted
away from education initiatives, the aging American infrastructure,
medical programs, and energy research. As the wars in Iraq and Afghanistan rage on, the U.S. military is likely to increase the demands
placed upon schools, teachers, and students. The costs of maintaining
a global military presence and simultaneously fighting two protracted
wars will contribute to a spiraling national debt, further weakening
the U.S. economy. Taken together, these forces threaten our standard
of living, tarnish our international image, and undermine our democratic institutions.

CONCLUSION

History educators are positioned at the intersection of ideological forces that seek to simplify the past and their mission to teach students about the complex world of historical study. This book explores the political forces that shape classroom teaching and the way we understand the Vietnam War. If the nation has not reached consensus about the meaning and lessons to be drawn from the use of nuclear weapons in World War II and the meaning of the Vietnam War, what can we expect from our children's high school textbooks? Does the selective tradition influence textbook narratives and present history in a way that uncritically endorses war-making? Or can we expect textbook publishers to take a more nuanced approach by acknowledging controversy, highlighting key evidence, and providing opportunities for students to evaluate the historical record for themselves? The answers to these questions may reveal much about what American students are taught about American wars, their civic responsibilities in relation to war, as well as possibilities for teaching critically about past and present U.S. military actions. Before addressing these questions, however, it is necessary to attend to the political and economic forces that shape textbook production, the history curriculum, and school policy.

CHAPTER 2

Whose History Is It?
A Close Look
at the
Corporate
Textbook

In March 2007, Dr. Richard Smith, former editor of the *British Medical Journal* and Chief Executive of United Healthcare Europe, called for the international medical community to stop contributing research to *The Lancet*, the world's premier journal of public health. *The Lancet,* published by the multinational media conglomerate Reed Elsevier, has printed articles critical of the tobacco industry, pharmaceutical companies, weapons manufacturers, and a number of studies on the effects military conflict has on the civilian populations of underdeveloped nations. Smith's call for a boycott of *The Lancet* stemmed from what he believed was a contradiction between *The Lancet's* readers', editors', and contributors' commitment to promoting public health and Reed Elsevier's active involvement in the global arms trade, through its subsidiary Reed Exhibitions, which sponsors arms fairs in Britain, the United States, the Middle East, Brazil, Germany, and Taiwan. Of particular concern to Smith was Reed Exhibition's promotion of cluster bombs known to kill civilians and torture devices manufactured by Security Equipment Corporation, whose slogan is "Making Grown Men Cry Since 1975" (Smith, 2007, p. 1).

Reed Elsevier's duplicitous stance in publishing public health journals while simultaneously profiting from the destruction of human life is emblematic of the prevailing economic climate of neoliberalism where professional ethics and the public good are subordinate to the creation of new markets and the perpetual pursuit of profit. Saltman (2004) explains that

> proponents of neoliberal ideology celebrate market solutions to all individual and social problems, advocate the privatization of goods and services and the liberalization of trade, and call for dismantling regulatory and social service dimensions of the state, which only interfere with the natural tendency of the market to benefit everybody. (p. 157)

The corporate encroachment on public space and influence on public policy can be observed in many aspects of American life. Pharmaceutical manufacturers and HMOs employ corporate lobbyists to influence health-care policy and secure passage of potentially dangerous drugs. Over the past 3 decades, incarceration has become a billion-dollar industry with its own trade newspaper (*Correctional Building News*), annual conventions, websites, trade shows, and mail-order catalogs (Schlosser, 1998, p. 3). Prisons are designed, built, and managed by private companies like KMD Architects, Turner Construction, and Corrections Corporation of America that lobby for tough sentencing guidelines responsible for placing more than 2.2 million Americans (half of whom are nonviolent offenders) behind bars (Fernandes, 2007; U.S. Department of Justice, 2008). This corporate influence over our corrections system creates potential for abuse. In 2009, judges Mark Ciavarella and Michael Conahan admitted to taking $2.6 million in bribes from a privately owned youth detention center in return for imposing extended sentences on thousands of children accused of minor crimes (Hurdle, 2009).

This trend toward privatizing social services can be seen in the military as well. The American occupation of Iraq and the "war on terrorism" have funneled billions of American tax dollars to corporations like Haliburton, which provides logistic support and material resources, and Blackwater, a private security company not bound by international law. In 2007, the U.S. government outsourced vital operations to more than 180,000 private contractors (while fighting the war with 163,100 U.S. military personnel) to rebuild infrastructure, provide security, collect intelligence, and transport supplies (Lardner,

2007). Within this era of neoliberalism, private corporations have also set out to secure new markets and maximize profits by encroaching upon one of the last viable public institutions: public schools.

THE CORPORATIZATION OF SCHOOLING

As a classroom teacher of more than a decade, I have seen the corporatization of schools manifest itself in three forms. In the first form corporations use teachers and/or students to create a spectacle to purify their public image and conceal the true nature of their business and/or product. For instance, McDonald's, the world's largest fast-food restaurant, has sponsored since 1979 the All-American basketball game, showcasing the top high school players in the nation. In an effort to improve its public image, the world's largest retailer, Wal-Mart, whose image has been tarnished by allegations of using child and illegal labor, gender discrimination, and failing to provide its employees with health insurance and living wages, awards $1,000 to a local school and gives a recognized teacher a $100 gift card. Exxon Mobil's Pegasus Awards Program provides $100,000 in school grants to support science, technology, engineering, and math. Defense contractor Lockheed Martin, the world's leading weapons manufacturer, sponsors science and engineering fairs in high schools throughout the nation.

The second form of school corporatization is when big businesses make agreements with local schools to promote and sell their products to a "captive" student audience (Apple, 2000). Coca-Cola and Pepsi provide school districts with funds for athletic facilities in exchange for exclusive pouring rights in cafeterias, faculty lounges, and extracurricular events. Dominos has a National School Lunch Program whereby local franchises deliver large volumes of discounted pizzas for consumption in the lunch rooms. Channel 1, a corporate program, provides public schools with electronics equipment in exchange for classroom time where teachers show students 12-minute news broadcasts embedded with corporate advertisements.

The third form of corporatism takes place when local school officials surrender various aspects of school governance (e.g., curriculum development, assessment, retention programs) to corporations that promise efficiency and academic achievement. Edison Schools, a private for-profit corporation, currently provides assessment, tutoring, and remediation services to 285,000 students in 97 schools in 19 states, Washington, D.C., and the United Kingdom (Edison Schools Inc., 2009, para. 3). McREL (Mid-continent Research for Education and Learning) works with Midwestern states in meeting the demands of No Child Left Behind by offering services that include auditing curricular implementation, aligning teaching with curricular standards, the sale of fully scripted classroom lessons and units, and a variety of after-school programs. Pearson, a textbook publisher with a global reach, offers Pearson Perpsective, a software program that tracks student performance on standardized exams, identifies incorrect responses, and provides customized online study guides designed to boost test scores and reduce attrition rates.

While most forms of corporatization can be observed and studied in their local context, corporate control of the textbook market can be studied on the national level. Textbook publishing is a global enterprise and perhaps the most lucrative of all school markets. In 2007, net sales of K–12 textbooks and ancillary materials amounted to approximately $6.3 billion. This represents 25% of the U.S. publishing industry's total net sales (Association of American Publishers, 2007). In the past 2 decades the textbook market has experienced intense consolidation, where four international multimedia conglomerates (Pearson, McGraw-Hill, Reed Elsevier, and Houghton Mifflin Harcourt) dominate the elementary-high school (commonly referred to as el-hi) publishing market (Sewall, 2005). The nation's leading publisher, Houghton Mifflin Harcourt, creates textbooks, teaching guides, audiovisual materials, computer software, standardized tests, and online assessment systems. McGraw-Hill, another leading textbook publisher with outlets in Asia, Australia, Europe, South America, and the United States and Canada, owns ABC television broadcasting affiliates in Colorado, California, and Indiana, and also owns Standard and Poor's and J.D. Power and Associates. Pearson is a London-based corporation that owns the Financial Times Group and Penguin Books, and has recently acquired textbook companies Addison-Wesley, Allyn and Bacon, Heinemann, Longman, Prentice Hall, and Silver Burdett. Reed Elsevier, global publisher of books, magazines, and science and medical journals, and the owner of Reed Exhibitions (discussed above) is also a leading textbook publisher and digital information provider.

These four large publishing corporations have created a production and distribution system that makes it difficult if not impossible for smaller publishers to enter the market. Drawing from a substantive pool of capital, these large publishing corporations create multiple editions of a single textbook, each designed to support a particular state's curricular framework and learning standards. In their quest to protect their access to the lucrative el-hi textbook market, textbook publishers formed the School Division of the Association of American

Publishers, a special interest group that actively lobbies state governments to increase public funding for curricular materials, promotes standards-based school reform initiatives, and works directly with state and local officials to ensure that textbooks make it on state adoption lists. In this next section, I closely examine the process by which textbooks are produced and adopted. By focusing on production and adoption, I throw into relief the two seemingly contradictory aims of corporate publisher devoted to profit and the public schools' mission to educate children to be thoughtful, critical citizens devoted to the common good.

THE CORPORATE TEXTBOOK PRODUCTION PROCESS

In contrast to academic writing designed to contribute to a particular field of study by asking new questions of the historical record, reporting new evidence, challenging orthodox interpretations, or taking up new perspectives, textbook writing is a corporate venture where publishers tightly control the production and marketing processes to ensure adoption and substantial profit. Young (1990), who worked as a freelance textbook editor and developer of instructional materials from 1978 to 1986, explains that the textbook production process consists of three phases: (1) preproduction, (2) development, and (3) postproduction. In the preproduction phase, publishing houses review sales figures, identify possible authors, examine competing textbooks, create focus group surveys to determine what teachers and administrators desire, and decide whether revising or creating a new textbook is cost-effective. The development phase includes choosing an author, creating a manuscript that meets curricular guidelines, hiring teacher-consultants to evaluate the pedagogical aspects of the textbook, commissioning experts to examine the content, and hiring editors to review information provided by consultants, surveys, focus groups, and salespeople. In the postproduction phase, sales figures are reviewed, publishing representatives are sent to professional gatherings to promote the textbook, and salespeople and consultants train teachers to use the textbook.

The production process raises questions about who is ultimately responsible for what appears in high school textbooks. This study includes four widely distributed textbooks that do not have authors, only committees of contributors and in-house writers. In some cases, textbook companies recruit a well-known expert in education or a particular field to sign on as the author *after* the textbook is completed

(Ansary, 2004, p. 31). When authors are involved in the early phases of production, it is standard procedure for publishing houses to require authors to sign a contract denying them authority over graphics, editorial revisions, and subsequent editions (Tyson-Bernstein, 1988). Mark Lytle, author of the textbook *A History of the Republic*, explains that once the first edition is released the author is reduced to a "kind of authentication role" where the publisher retains the right to introduce new material and update textbooks by incorporating new teaching methods, artwork, and designs (Lytle, 1993, as cited in Loewen, 1996, p. 283).

There is also evidence suggesting that in an effort to improve sales, textbook companies have pressured authors to revise content and design. In a now dated, but revealing essay on the trials of writing high school history textbooks, Henry Bragdon (1969), author of Macmillan's *History of a Free People*, explains that although his publisher generally gave him a great deal of freedom, political factors did influence the final narrative. For instance, his editor insisted on the Civil War being called the War Between the States. He describes his reaction to this stipulation:

> This concession to the Southern market irritated me, and I demanded that Macmillan prove it was necessary. So they polled their eleven southern sales offices; every one of them solemnly stated that a textbook that used the term Civil War could not be sold south of the Mason-Dixon line. I gave in. Texas, I thought, was worth a mass. This is one occasion where the publishers in effect forced me to do something I disliked. (Bragdon, 1969, p. 293)

Bragdon is not the only textbook author whom corporate editors have pressured to rewrite the narrative. When the Ginn Corporation noticed that sales of Boorstin and Kelley's (two noted conservative historians) *A History of the United States* (1983) were lower than projected, a team of editors and marketing experts were assembled to revise the textbook and produce a more profitable second edition. (Ginn Corporation was the original publisher of their textbook. Prentice Hall absorbed it in 1988 and is now owned by Pearson.) The team determined that the reading level was too high for high school students and questioned what they believed were elements of elitism, racism, and antifeminism. Boorstin and Kelley insisted that the narrative reflected their professional bias, not prejudice, and that the integrity of the textbook be preserved. Although they rejected their editors' requests to add charts, graphs, focus questions, or change the two-column format, Ginn Corporation did persuade the authors to significantly revise passages on slavery, the Civil Rights era, the New Left, and the Feminist movement (O'Brien, 1989).

Like any corporate product line, whether it be automobiles, cosmetics, or iPods, textbook corporations work to keep their products competitive at minimal cost. Successful textbooks are well known and brand name matters. This means that textbook narratives are continuously revised, but never completely rewritten. For instance, Lewis Paul Todd and Merle Curti's *Rise of the American Nation,* published between 1950 and 1982, was revised several times after one author died and the other resided in a nursing home (Schemo, 2006, p. 2). Today, Paul Boyer (a noted U.S. historian and professor emeritus at the University of Wisconsin) is credited as the author for the most recent edition of this textbook, entitled *The American Nation.* In 2007 I contacted him asking about the peculiar relationship between authors and textbook publishers. His response is worth quoting at length:

> I inherited the authorship of *The American Nation* from Merle Curti, the original author of *Rise of the American Nation,* first published by Harcourt Brace in the 1950s, and a collaborator he later took on, his former student Lewis Paul Todd. This was a congenial transition process, since Merle Curti was an emeritus professor of history here at Wisconsin when I arrived in 1980, and despite the generational difference, he and I became close personal friends. He was always very supportive as the transition was made from his authorship to mine.
>
> I provide this background to make clear that I did not write this textbook originally, but inherited a work that was already well established. So my role has been with tweaking successive revisions and, of course, handling the recent events that must be covered in each new edition. The work on new editions is a collaborative process involving in-house editors and myself as author. Some passages I draft and some are initially drafted by in-house editors at Holt, Rinehart & Winston's offices in Austin, sent to me for my revision and correction. I read everything, making changes and correction ranging from details of fact and matters of style to substantive interpretive issues. I worked very closely with an HRW editor in preparing an insert that was added to the current edition covering the run-up to the Iraq War, making sure that we gave attention to the critics of the rush to war such as Senator Byrd of West Virginia, as well as to the Administration's case. (This was well before the Administration's case for war had been as totally discredited as it now is.) (P. Boyer, personal communication, August 12, 2007)

While Boyer's active involvement in rewriting the narrative and up-dating subsequent editions is notable, some publishing houses choose to minimize production costs by maintaining complete control over narrative, creating awkward situations for both publishers and cred-ited authors. In 2006, James Loewen, author *of Lies My Teacher Told Me*, discovered that Pearson Prentice Hall produced two textbooks that featured nearly identical passages on 9/11, the presidential election of 2000, the Persian Gulf War, the war in Afghanistan, and the cre-ation of the Department of Homeland Security. This was problematic in that Daniel J. Boorstin and Brooks Mather Kelley are credited as the authors of one of the books, *A History of the United States*; while Alan Winkler, Andrew Cayton, Elisabeth Perry, and Linda Reed are credited as authors of the other textbook, *America: Pathways to the Present*. In their rush to include these critical events and minimize productions costs, Pearson Prentice Hall appears to have inserted the same passage. When asked about the nearly identical passages, Allan Winkler, a pro-fessor of history at the University of Miami of Ohio, explained that he did not write the passages and that the situation was "embarrassing" and "inexcusable" (Schemo, 2006, p. 2).

THE TEXTBOOK ADOPTION PROCESS

Publishing houses tightly control the production process and their hired writers primarily because they appreciate the complexity of the U.S. school market. The U.S. textbook market is divided into open and closed territories. Most of the Northeast, Midwest, and West are considered open territories where textbook companies sell directly to school districts. Each district in open states has different criteria and procedures guiding the adoption process. Publishing companies devel-op textbooks for the larger open states such as New York, where text-book packages are designed to support state standards. For instance, the first 48 pages of the New York State version of McDougal Littell's *World History: Patterns of Interaction,* features a correlation guide listing the historical content outlined by the New York State social studies curricula followed by a list of pages where that content can be found in the textbook. Textbook representatives use this feature as a selling point for teachers and administrators pressured to continuously raise test scores.

Textbook companies devote approximately 24% of publishing and operating expenses to selling and marketing (Association of American Publishers [AAP], 2007, p. 35). This money is used to pay textbook salespeople who work in open states to build new accounts and maintain ties to schools. In an effort to edge out the competition, textbook companies sponsor educational conferences, treat teachers and administrators to faculty dinners, and provide free classroom materials. When school budgets are tight, large textbook companies have been willing to allow school districts to buy books on credit.

With the exception of the larger open states like New York, Illinois, Michigan, and New Jersey, textbook publishers devote much of their time and resources attending to the 22 states that are considered "closed territories." The 22 adoption states are Alabama, Arkansas, California, Florida, Georgia, Idaho, Indiana, Kentucky, Louisiana, Mississippi, Nevada, New Mexico, North Carolina, Oklahoma, Oregon, South Carolina, Tennessee, Texas, Utah, Virginia, and West Virginia (AAP, 2007). These are "adoption states," where school districts select their textbooks from a state list of approved textbooks. Textbook adoptions coincide with the 6-year cycle of rewriting state-learning frameworks. To ensure a place on adoption lists, publishers consult state guidelines when writing textbooks. If a textbook is adopted, it will be one of a lucky few purchased in closed states. Once a textbook is passed over by a state adoption committee, it is not considered for another 6 years. To gain access to the nation's largest markets, textbook companies attend to highly populated adoption states like California, Florida, and Texas. These 3 states have a combined population of approximately 13 million students, while the next 18 adoption states combined have roughly 12.7 million (Ansary, 2004, p. 33). Texas is the most influential of the big three adoption states. It is the only state that designates a huge amount of money exclusively for purchasing textbooks. This money must be spent in an adoption year. Whereas California approves textbooks for K–8, Texas approves every textbook for grades K–12. This creates what textbook publishers call the "Texas" or "California" effect, where publishers design textbooks that meet the larger states' curricula (Tulley & Farr, 1990, p. 166). Sewall (2005) explains, "If the TEKS [Texas Essential Knowledge and Skills] specifically mentions South Africa's Desmond Tutu, for example as it did in 2001, it is guaranteed that Desmond Tutu will obtain a prominent position in new [textbook] editions. If a largely unknown figure in antiquity, Eratosthenes, appears on the TEKS list, he too will flourish" (p. 502).

The TEKS Social Studies Curriculum for High School is a list of historical events to be learned by rote memorization, explanation, and concept analysis. The word "understands" appears 121 times (e.g., "The student understands the impact of totalitarianism in the 20th century"), "identify" appears 95 times (e.g., identify and explain causes and effects of World Wars I and II), and "analyze" 122 times (e.g., analyze the nature of totalitarian regimes in China, Nazi Germany, and the Soviet Union). Repeatedly understanding, identifying, and analyzing a predetermined body of historical fragments passes as historical knowledge. By treating history as a static entity comprised of technical knowledge compartmentalized into a series of units, TEKS represents Freire's banking concept of education. In this system, students are treated as empty containers to be filled by teachers and "education becomes the act of depositing, in which students are the depositories and the teacher is the depositor. Instead of communicating, the teacher issues communiqués and makes deposits students patently receive, memorize, and repeat" (Freire, 1993, p. 53).

The adoption process is problematic in that political interest groups influence the adoption process. California and Texas are home to a variety of liberal and conservative groups that contest textbook treatments of evolution, sex education, homosexuality, history, and most recently, climate change. After reviewing textbooks and hearing concerns from political advocacy groups, state adoption committees can approve them, reject them, or suggest revisions. In the 1980s and 1990s, Christian conservatives Mel and Norma Gabler of Educational Research Analysts successfully influenced the Texas Board of Education to "eliminate material they consider unpatriotic, socialistic, communistic, humanistic, anti-religious, anti-creationist, anti-authoritarian, and anti-family" (Delfattore, 1992, p. 140). When the Gablers (who incidentally do not hold college degrees) encountered a social studies textbook that read, "These [New Deal] programs and policies were generally successful in restoring the prosperity of many Americans," they successfully lobbied the Texas Board of Education to request that the publisher change the sentence to, "In spite of this, by the time the United States entered World War II, most of the nation was still suffering from the Great Depression" (p. 149). After being written into textbooks designed to be picked up in Texas, these revisions then become part of textbooks sold in other states.

Private corporations are also actively involved in evaluating and revising textbooks to reflect business interests. In 2002, Duggan Flanakin, who was previously employed by the U.S. Bureau of Mines, wrote a series of textbook reports for the conservative Texas Public Policy Foundation. He was involved in approving a textbook entitled *Global Science: Energy, Resources, Environment*, published by Kendall/Hunt and underwritten by the Mineral Information Institute, an association of mining companies. Another textbook, *Environmental Science:*

How the World Works and Your Place in It was initially rejected by the state board and eventually approved only after the publisher revised the book to meet criticisms leveled by the Texas Public Policy Foundation. The sentence "Destruction of the tropical rain forest could affect weather over the entire planet" was revised to "Tropical rain forest ecosystems impact weather over the entire planet." The publisher also inserted the passage, "In the past the earth has been much warmer than it is now, and fossils of sea creatures show us that the sea level was much higher than it is today. So does it really matter if the earth gets warmer?" (Stille, 2002, p. 2).

The bottom line is that textbooks are designed, written, revised, and marketed to be apolitical, a quality that ensures state adoption and high sales. Tamim Ansary, a former editor at Harcourt Brace Jovanovich who has written textbooks for Houghton Mifflin, McDougall Littell, and Prentice Hall, explains that textbook publishers, careful not to offend the right or left, cleanse textbooks of content that might be considered objectionable, effectively censoring themselves (Ansary, 2004, p. 35). To accomplish this, large publishing houses develop hundreds of pages of guidelines and checklists used to purge textbooks of photos, phrases, or resources that may draw negative attention. The end result is the production, adoption, and dissemination of textbook narratives scrubbed of controversy, new research, and alternative perspectives, a vital part of historical study and democratic life.

THE CONNECTION BETWEEN
TEXTBOOKS AND STANDARDS-BASED EDUCATION

The production process and adoption system compromise textbook quality. Regardless of their historical quality, textbook net sales have increased $300 million from $5.8 billion in 2002 to $6.1 billion in 2008 (AAP, 2009, p. 2). In an era of standardized curricula and high-stakes testing, textbooks are invaluable for teachers responsible for covering hundreds of curricular topics, and administrators pressured to continuously raise standardized test scores. At the time of this writing, all 50 states have developed academic standards for core subjects (Quality Counts, 2008, p. 7). The standards movement, predicated on a positivistic view of learning that treats knowledge as a static entity, operates under the assumption that a battery of paper and pencil exams can be used to accurately measure learning, evaluate academic programs, and ultimately improve education achievement (Mathison & Ross, 2004). Test results, which are highly correlated with parental income and race, are used to define academic achievement (Sacks, 2001). In the quest for accountability, state education departments maintain databases to monitor standardized test results and determine which schools are in good standing, those in need of improvement, and in extreme cases, those to be closed.

Standards-Based Learning and Classroom Instruction

Standards-based learning is an educational juggernaut that redefines the way we think about teaching, learning, and school reform. The language of benchmarks, performance goals, and adequate yearly progress drives district initiatives, permeates faculty meetings, and dominates departmental goals. The use of test scores as the sole indication of instructional quality vitiates democratic reform and quality school relationships based on trust and mutual respect. Local school officials, parents, and teachers are precluded from defining and assessing local programs or generating policies that meet local needs. The authoritarian world of standards education pits stakeholders against one another: the state pressures administrators to make adequate progress (read: raising test scores), administrators pressure teachers to align instruction with state curricula (read: teach to the test), and classroom teachers coerce students to quietly endure rote instruction and faithfully perform a series of simple exercises on paper and pencil tests.

Standardized social studies instruction undermines authentic instruction and open-ended inquiry where students are encouraged to explore the historical record, critically analyze information, conduct research, examine public policies, or solve problems. In standards-based structures, external authorities determine learning outcomes in advance, and the only knowledge that counts is that which can be measured on paper and pencil tests. For instance, the New York State Core Curriculum for Social Studies provides teachers with a comprehensive outline of historical content, major themes, and a list of cross-curricular connections. This curriculum rigidly organizes world history into eight units (e.g., Unit One: Ancient World—Civilizations and Religion), 51 general topics (e.g., World War II—causes and effects), and 280 subtopics (e.g., India—independence and partition) (New York State Education Department [NYSED], 1999, pp. 45–77). The vast number of concepts to be taught, learned, and assessed fosters instructional decisions that emphasize mechanistic, rote instruction and moving quickly from one topic to the next. For example, when teaching about the Roman Empire, there is no time for freely exploring Rome's cultural achievements, critically examining Roman political and social institutions, and evaluating the positive and negative effects of imperial rule. Rather, to be knowledgeable about the Roman Empire is to know its geography, the factors leading to its growth, its achievements, and the forces that precipitated its decline (NYSED, 1999, p. 97). Deviating from this script leaves less time for teaching other topics. The end result is that "subject matter becomes *hypersimplified*, denatured to the point that it exists only as a collection of mere facts or rote ideas useful for mechanized storage and retrieval. . . ." (Vinson, Gibson, & Ross, 2004, p. 83).

The entire system of standardized education relies on a culture of compliance where local school officials and teachers are compelled to carry out an educational system where the curricular content, pedagogical strategies, and methods of evaluation are determined by external authorities. Textbooks serve as the primary reference point for delivering the state curriculum. Accountability measures and standardized exams ensure that teachers who deviate from the prescribed ritual will be easily identified, corrected, and in some cases sanctioned. In the quest to boost test scores and avoid state sanctions, school districts conduct item analysis of past exams to determine where students missed questions and where teachers need to augment their instruction.

In addition to creating enormous pressure to "teach to the test," this combination of high-stakes testing and standardized curricula creates a curricular shell game that keeps teachers and administrators in a continual state of confusion, guessing what content will be on the next high-stakes test. This curricular shell game diverts precious time and resources away from crafting programs and policies that meet the local needs of the diverse student populations attending public schools. The end result is the creation of learning environments where authentic learning, free inquiry, and creative expression are considered irresponsible activities and the most talented, caring teachers will have their pedagogy reduced to a mechanistic ritual of high-paced direct instruction (Mabry, Poole, Redmond, & Schultz, 2003; Moon, Callahan, & Tomlinson, 2003).

From Textbooks to Test Booklets

Despite the very real flaws of standards-based learning initiatives strengthened by the No Child Left Behind Act, the School Division of the American Association of Publishers (which is comprised of textbook publishers) actively advocates standardized testing as the primary method of evaluating schools, a tool to improving teaching and learning, and a means to generate data to inform education policy. The School Division's stated purpose is to support the No Child Left Behind Act by working to "ensure all students have the opportunity to learn by having access to a wide variety of standards-based instructional content" (School Division of Association of American Publishers [SDAAP], 2009). To show its support for standards-based learning, in April 2007, McGraw-Hill, Harcourt Assessment, Pearson Education, Riverside Publishing, Data Recognition Corporation, and Scholastic Testing sponsored the School Division's creation of the website TestingFacts.org. Disguised as a resource to inform the public of the alleged benefits of standardized testing, TestingFacts.org is a corporate advertisement promoting high-stakes exams as valuable tools that support student learning, track school performance, and hold school leaders and teachers accountable for meeting academic standards.

Standards-based learning is a windfall for the publishing and testing industry. Textbook publishers and testing companies reap huge profits from state and federal polices like the No Child Left Behind Act that mandate children sit for a battery of standardized exams as they make their way from kindergarten to commencement. New York State, which has approximately 3 million students enrolled in grades K–12, administers some 17 standardized exams before students enter 9th grade (Abrams, 2008). Nationally, American schools administer approximately 45 million standardized tests a year (Education Sector, 2006). At an average cost of $3 per test, potential annual sales exceed $135,000,000. Kaplan, the biggest of the testing companies, was valued at $70 million in 1991; it is now worth $2 billion (Public Broadcasting System Nightly Business Report, 2008, para. 10).

Textbook companies have also fought for a piece of the lucrative testing market valued at $2.6 billion in 2007 (Public Broadcasting System Nightly Business Report, 2008). Riverside Publishing, a subsidiary of Houghton Mifflin Harcourt, currently has contracts for providing large-scale state assessments with the states of Arkansas, Georgia, Louisiana, Mississippi, Missouri, New York, Nevada, Oklahoma, South Carolina, and Utah. In addition to creating textbooks and tests, textbook companies reap profits from student workbooks, test prep materials, and classroom resources. Riverside has also opened up new streams of revenue by providing scoring services that relieve local schools of the burden of finding the time and resources to grade exams. For the widely administered IOWA tests, Riverside provides schools with lists of student scores with class, building, and system summaries ($0.23 per student); student labels ($0.70 per student); student snapshot reports ($0.29 per student); class snapshot reports ($0.18 per student); building snapshot reports ($0.18 per student); and even item analyses ($0.25 per student) detailing the questions that a cohort answered correctly and incorrectly (Riverside Publishing, 2009, p. 3). It is difficult to imagine a system of education that could present more economic opportunities to the multinational conglomerates that influence educational policy and dominate the American textbook and testing industry.

CONCLUSION

When we consider that the social studies' purpose is to "help young people develop the ability to make informed and reasoned decisions for the public good as citizens of a culturally diverse, democratic society in an interdependent world," history textbooks seem to be rather peculiar pedagogical devices (National Council for the Social Studies [NCSS], 1994, p. vii). The corporatization of schooling, market-driven production process, and the flawed adoption system indicate that textbooks represent publishing companies' best efforts to use cost-effective processes and marketing strategies to create attractive yet noncontroversial textbooks that appeal to teachers, appease political interest groups, and meet state adoption committees' criteria. Regardless of quality, publishing houses profit from a commercial system of education that ultimately degrades teaching and learning. Much like the contradictions created by Reed's publication of *The Lancet* and its partnership with arms manufacturers, the size of these corporations, vastness of their holdings, and active promotion of high-stakes testing create conflicts of interest between the quest for increasing profits and the best interests of schools, communities, and children. Having highlighted the political influences on the social studies curriculum and the corporatization of the textbook industry, I now explore leading textbook narratives, the point at which these forces intersect. In the next two chapters I take a close look at the leading textbooks treatment of the Gulf of Tonkin crisis and Tet Offensive, perhaps the two most critical (and controversial) events of the Vietnam War.

CHAPTER 3

A Patriotic Rendering of the Gulf of Tonkin Crisis

In a late-night television address on August 4, 1964, President Lyndon Johnson informed the American public that a crisis was developing in the Gulf of Tonkin. In this broadcast Johnson declared "It is my duty to the American people to report that renewed hostile actions against United States ships on the high seas in the Gulf of Tonkin have today required me to order the military forces of the United States to take action in reply" (Johnson, 1964, online). In concluding his address, Johnson explained that he had met with congressional leaders and would request a resolution authorizing him to take "all necessary measures in support of freedom and in defense of peace in Southeast Asia" (p. 1). American newspapers supported the president. On August 7, the *New York Times* ran editorials from 27 American newspapers. Twenty-four supported the bombings without reservation, two expressed slight reservations, and one was noncommittal (Aronson, 1970, p. 219). What the president did not reveal, and what the newspapers disregarded, was that the United States had been waging a covert war against North Vietnam for months prior to the incident, the alleged attacks of August 4th were never confirmed, and Johnson had a resolution to expand the war drawn up months before August 1964.

Although more than 40 years has passed since the Gulf of Tonkin crisis, high school history textbooks have failed to challenge Johnson's account of what transpired in the Gulf of Tonkin in August 1964. Since 1964, myriad government reports, historical accounts, and eyewitness testimonies have strongly suggested that U.S. government officials used the attacks in the Gulf of Tonkin as a pretext to escalate the Vietnam War. In what follows, I focus my analysis on the United States' covert war against North Vietnam in the spring and summer of 1964, the events of August 2 and 4, and the passage of the Gulf of Tonkin Resolution. As I review these events, I closely examine how high school history textbooks compare to major historical accounts written on the Gulf of Tonkin crisis.

THE UNITED STATES PREPARES TO ESCALATE THE VIETNAM WAR

Nineteen sixty-three was a disastrous year for the United States' mission to contain communism in Southeast Asia. The Viet Cong (a homegrown, largely independent South Vietnamese insurgent movement) were growing in number. Buddhist monks were attracting international attention for their well-organized protests against Ngo Din Diem's oppressive and brutal South Vietnamese government. Plagued by corruption, South Vietnam's military, the Army of the Republic of Vietnam (ARVN), proved to be ineffective fighting the Viet Cong. In the fall of 1963, with President Kennedy's approval, a military junta assassinated Diem, who ruled South Vietnam with American support for nearly a decade. In December 1963, Secretary of Defense Robert McNamara reported that South Vietnam's government was weakening, its military was plagued by desertions, the U.S. strategic hamlet program was overextended, and the Viet Cong were growing in strength and influence. Concerned with "falling dominoes," McNamara indicated that a plan for covert action into North Vietnam was being devised and would include "a wide variety of sabotage and psychological operations against North Vietnam . . . that provide maximum pressure with minimum risk" (Sheehan et al., 1971, p. 273). He concluded his pessimistic report by advising, "We should watch the situation very carefully, running scared, hoping for the best, but preparing for more forceful moves if the situation does not show early signs of improvement" (Sheehan et al., 1971, p. 274).

May 1964 proved a decisive month for the United States in Vietnam. On May 4, South Vietnam's General Nguyen Khanh, who gained control of South Vietnam, with American support, after Diem's assassination, requested that the United States place South Vietnam on a war footing. Convinced Hanoi was aiding the Viet Cong insurgency, Khanh asked 10,000 U.S. Special Forces to be dispatched to South Vietnam and urged the United States to consider making a formal declaration of war against North Vietnam (Sheehan et al., 1971, p. 246). Initially Khan's requests received a cool response from Washington. However, just 2 weeks later, in the neighboring country of Laos, the pro-communist Pathet Lao launched an attack against Prince Souvanna Phouma's pro-American government. This offensive resulted in communist forces controlling a significant portion of the Plaine des Jarres, located in Thailand's central highlands. Underscoring the importance of Laos to the United States' larger mission to contain communism in Southeast Asia, the Pentagon historians wrote, "These developments lent a greater sense of urgency to the arguments of those advisers favoring prompt measures to strengthen the U.S. position in Southeast Asia" (*The Pentagon Papers*, 1971a, p. 165).

Developing a Blueprint for War

Seriously concerned about South Vietnam's weakening government, the growing Viet Cong insurgency, and losing Laos, the White House quickly developed a blueprint for expanding the war into North Vietnam. William Bundy, President Johnson's Assistant Secretary of State for Far Eastern Affairs, drafted a 30-day graduated program of political and military maneuvers that would pave the way for the United States to openly attack North Vietnam. After the initial 10 days, this program included obtaining a joint resolution from Congress (20 days before, or D –20), requesting political support from the United Kingdom, Australia, New Zealand, and Pakistan (D –14), moving U.S. forces in position for air strikes (D –12), informing the U.S. public of a possible strike (D –3), and removing dependents and launching air strikes (D-day) (Sheehan et al., 1971, pp. 248–249). In conjunction with the 30-day scenario, Bundy also drafted a congressional resolution authorizing the president to use force to defend any Southeast Asian nation that was threatened by communist aggression. On June 1 and 2 the Joint Chiefs of Staff produced a preliminary draft of what would become a comprehensive list of 94 North Vietnamese military and industrial targets that could (and would) be drawn upon in a crisis (Sheehan et al., 1971, p. 251). Thus, by the summer of 1964, the White House and the Pentagon had achieved consensus that the United States would be in position to expand its military efforts to defeat communism in Southeast Asia.

In conjunction with Washington's plans to expand the war, U.S. forces in South Vietnam initiated a covert war, code-named OPLAN 34A, against North Vietnam on February 1, 1964. Neil Sheehan explains that

> Through 1964, the 34A operations ranged from flights over North Vietnam by U-2 spy planes and kidnappings of North Vietnamese citizens for intelligence information, to parachuting sabotage and psychological warfare teams into the North, commando raids from the sea to blow up rail and highway bridges, and the bombardment of North Vietnamese coastal installations by PT [patrol torpedo] boats. (Sheehan et al., 1971, p. 238)

The coastal raids carried out as part of OPLAN 34A were used to provoke a North Vietnamese response and serve as a pretext to widen the war. Daniel Ellsberg (2002) describes what he learned about OPLAN 34A raids while working in the Pentagon in 1964 under Assistant Secretary of Defense John McNaughton:

> They were entirely U.S. operations, code-named 34A ops. . . . For the raids against North Vietnam, of which Hanoi had publicly complained, the United States owned the fast patrol boats known as Nastys (which the CIA had purchased from Norway), hired the crews, and controlled every aspect of the operations. The CIA ran the training, with help from the U.S. Navy, and recruited the crews; some of them were recruited, as individuals, from the South Vietnamese Navy, others were CIA "assets" from Taiwan and elsewhere in Asia, along with mercenaries from around the world. (Ellsberg, 2002, p. 14)

Ellsberg is not the only one to grasp the fact that 34A raids were essentially U.S. raids conducted to apply pressure on North Vietnam. Gulf of Tonkin historian Edwin Moise suggested that the North Vietnamese also "understood the fundamental nature of these raids: they were carried out by Vietnamese personnel working as agents of American policy" (Moise, 1996, p. 57).

The U.S. Covert War Against North Vietnam

None of the textbooks make any direct reference to Johnson's plans to escalate the war. Although these preparations for escalation are included in scholarly accounts of the war (Duiker, 1994, p. 319; Herring, 2002a, pp. 141–142; Karnow, 1997, p. 376; Logevall, 1999, pp. 122–129), high school textbooks have effectively stricken the spring of 1964 from the historical record. In its place, the high school history textbooks offer two different types of narratives. The first type of narrative highlights the precariousness of South Vietnam's government but fails to mention U.S. preparations to expand the war. The second type of narrative evades the topic of South Vietnamese instability and merely informs students that the Gulf of Tonkin crisis was part of the larger Cold War hostilities.

In developing the first narrative, several of the American history and world history textbooks highlight that South Vietnam was plagued with problems in 1964 and ignore U.S. preparations to expand the war. For example, *The American Vision*, describing the period after Diem's assassination, asserts, "the [South Vietnamese] government grew increasingly weak and unstable. The United States became even more deeply involved in order to prop up the weak South Vietnamese government" (Appleby et al., 2005, p. 898). Gary Nash's *American Odyssey* offers a similar statement: "By 1964 . . . Diem's successors had proved just as unsuccessful in waging the war and just as unpopular with the South Vietnamese. Only massive military aid from the United States would keep the regime from toppling" (Nash, 2002, p. 772).

Likewise, four of the world history textbooks, *Patterns of Interaction, Connections to Today, The Human Journey,* and *Continuity and Change* ignore the political and military failings of South Vietnam and, by association, the United States. These textbooks limit their narratives to Cold War rhetoric, attributing the United States' commitment to South Vietnam as part of a measure taken to contain communism and prevent countries surrounding South Vietnam from falling. For instance, *A History of the United States* does not include any information about Viet Cong advances, McNamara's pessimistic reports, or Diem's largely ineffective successor Nguyen Khanh. Rather than citing the growing problems in Vietnam, the textbook's authors draw upon Cold War rhetoric: "Secretary of State Dean Rusk said that just as our duties to the free world required us to stay in Berlin—so we must defend freedom in Vietnam" (p. 809). In a similar fashion, *The Human Experience* prefaces its treatment of the Gulf of Tonkin crisis by explaining, "Since the early 1950s, American officials had accepted the domino theory—that if one Southeast Asian land fell to communism, its neighbors would fall as well" (Farah & Karls, 1999, p. 911).

By limiting the narratives to Cold War rhetoric, the textbooks hide from students the fact that the United States was losing its struggle to contain communism, its proxy government and army were on the brink of ruin, and the Viet Cong were growing in strength and numbers.

Students are not informed that these unfortunate events compelled the Johnson administration to take an aggressive stance and make preparations for war. Even more troubling is that the textbooks fail to mention that, in conjunction with these plans, the United States was effectively waging a covert war against North Vietnam months before the Gulf of Tonkin crisis in August of 1964. Whereby historians consider U.S.-directed OPLAN 34A raids as a provocation that factored into the Gulf of Tonkin clash on August 2, they are ignored or grossly misrepresented in high school history textbooks. Instead, textbooks describe the OPLAN 34A raids as South Vietnamese operations merely *supported by* the United States. Here are several examples from the textbooks:

> Few Americans questioned the president's account of the incident. Years later, however, it was revealed that Johnson withheld the truth from the public and Congress. The American warships had been *helping* South Vietnamese commandos raid two North Vietnamese islands the night of the attacks. (Nash, 2002, p. 773, emphasis added)

> Johnson did not reveal that American warships had been *helping* the South Vietnamese conduct electronic spying and commando raids against North Vietnam. (Appleby et al., 2005, p. 898, emphasis added)

> Off North Vietnam in the Gulf of Tonkin on August 2 and 4, 1964, two United States destroyers were attacked by North Vietnamese gunboats. This brought matters to a head. President Johnson said they were attacked without cause. (Later it appeared that they had been *protecting South Vietnamese* gunboats making raids on the North.). (Boorstin & Kelley, 2005, p. 809, emphasis added)

> Johnson claimed that the attacks in the Gulf of Tonkin were unprovoked. In reality, however, the U.S. destroyer *Maddox* had been spying *in support of* South Vietnamese raids against North Vietnam and had fired first. (Boyer, 2005, p. 984, emphasis added)

Or, when the textbooks indicate that the United States was responsible for the raids, it is treated as an allegation, not a well-documented fact:

> On August 2, 1964 [*sic:* the announcement was actually made on August 4th], President Johnson announced that North Vietnamese torpedo boats had attacked two American destroyers, the USS *Maddox* and *C. Turner Joy*, which were patrolling in the Gulf of Tonkin off the North

Vietnamese coast. The North Vietnamese charged that the U.S. ships were conducting naval raids. Nonetheless, the North Vietnamese denied attacking the ships. (Danzer et al., 1998, p. 888)

Only one of the 12 textbooks, *The American Vision*, comes close to accurately depicting the OPLAN 34A raids. It is tucked away in a separate two-page section entitled "You're the Historian." This section offers 15 statements made between August 2 and 4 by Fulbright, Herrick, Johnson, McNamara, Rowan, and Rusk. The textbook quotes Rusk as saying, "We believe that the present OPLAN 34-A activities are beginning to rattle Hanoi [Capital of North Vietnam] and the *Maddox* incident is directly related to their effort to resist these activities. We have no intention of yielding to pressure" (Appleby et al., 2005, p. 902). After reading the quotes, students are presented with questions. The first question asks students to identify the statement by Rusk that "suggests the United States may have provoked the attack on the *Maddox*" (Appleby et al., 2005, p. 903). This exercise, void of any context or explanation and set apart from *The American Vision*'s main narrative (which confuses the August 2 skirmish with the alleged attacks of August 4), is the only place any of the 12 textbooks mentions OPLAN 34A raids.

The other 11 authors misrepresent the true relationship between Saigon and Washington. Washington was funding the war, supporting South Vietnam's weak economy with massive amounts of aid, and directing the covert raids. The textbooks lead students to believe that somehow the United States was following General Khanh's lead and merely offering assistance when, in reality, President Johnson and many members of his cabinet were fighting the war years before Washington policymakers agreed on General Khanh's installation. The narratives also divert students' attention away from the covert war the United States waged against North Vietnam prior to the Gulf of Tonkin incidents of August 2 and August 4. Although the textbook's authors devote space to other American operations that involved the South Vietnamese (e.g., the Pacification program and Vietnamization), there are no references, descriptions of, or maps illustrating the OPLAN 34A raids. Thus, the United States is made out to be defending itself against a communist aggressor. Students are not allowed to know that these raids were provocations that would serve as an American pretext for openly expanding the war into North Vietnam.

By ignoring South Vietnam's desperate political situation, largely misrepresenting OPLAN 34A raids, and treating U.S. provocations as unfounded accusations, the textbooks reflect the official government line. If the authors were interested in producing an accurate historical account supported by evidence, they would inform students that starting in February 1964, the United States initiated a secret war against North Vietnam code-named OPLAN 34A. This secret war was directed and funded by the United States and carried out by South Vietnamese forces or Asian mercenaries. In addition, this secret war included aerial attacks on the North Vietnamese military posts and maritime raids on North Vietnamese vessels, defense systems, and islands. Even if all the textbooks wished to achieve was balance (as opposed to accuracy), then they would at least allow students to hear what the North Vietnamese had to say about the affair. For instance, in a document entitled "Memorandum Regarding the U.S. War Acts Against the Democratic Republic of Vietnam in the First Days of August 1964," the DRV explained,

> In recent years, U.S. and South Vietnamese air and naval craft have repeatedly intruded into the airspace and the territorial waters of the Democratic Republic of Viet Nam, threatened the security of the population of the coastal regions, and smuggled in many commando groups for espionage and sabotage activities. . . . (Galloway, 1970, p. 498)

This statement is critically important as it corroborates the Pentagon historians' descriptions of American bombing and strafing of North Vietnamese frontier posts and villages and the shelling of islands and other targets located along North Vietnam's coastline. Although these events are considered to be important enough to be fully explored in scholarly accounts of the Gulf of Tonkin crisis (Moise's opening chapter is entitled "Covert Operations"), only one of the 12 textbooks even acknowledges the OPLAN 34A raids, or that the United States used these raids as a pretext to escalate war in Vietnam.

THE GULF OF TONKIN CRISIS

By August 1964, the situation in South Vietnam was continuing to deteriorate. On July 15, General Maxwell Taylor, who had been recently appointed ambassador to South Vietnam, reported the number of Viet Cong soldiers had increased from 28,000 to 34,000 (*The Pentagon Papers*, 1971a, p. 80). A week later, South Vietnam's General Khanh began pressuring the United States to initiate offensive operations against North Vietnam by publicly campaigning for a "march to the north" (p. 81).

In addition to South Vietnam's precarious situation, President Johnson learned that Senator Barry Goldwater had been nominated to represent the Republican Party in the upcoming presidential election. Goldwater, a general in the Air Force Reserve, was known for his staunch anticommunism and wasted no time attacking Johnson's Vietnam policies. In his acceptance speech, Goldwater criticized Johnson and McNamara for failing to articulate their plans for Vietnam:

> Make no bones of this. Don't try to sweep this under the rug. We are at war in Vietnam. And yet the president, who is commander-in-chief of our forces, refuses to say, mind you— whether the objective there is victory, and his Secretary of Defense continues to mislead and misinform the American people. . . . (Powers, 1964, as cited in Logevall, 1999, p. 195)

Resolved in his commitment to save South Vietnam, but confronted by South Vietnam's faltering government and the growing pressure to do something about it, Johnson elected to step up the covert raids. The Pentagon historians explain that the OPLAN 34A raids consisted of three phases designed to meet several objectives:

> (1) harassment; (2) diversion; (3) political pressure; (4) capture of prisoners; (5) physical destruction; (6) acquisition of intelligence; (7) generation of intelligence; and (8) diversion of DRV resources. (*The Pentagon Papers,* 1971a, pp. 150–151)

Phase I consisted of intelligence collection, leaflet drops, radio broadcasts, and small-scale maritime operations that would serve as "pinpricks" (pp. 150–153). In Phases II and III the same operations would intensify and "destructive undertakings" would be extended to targets associated with "North Vietnam's economic and industrial well-being" (p. 150). Logevall explains that this was a significant departure from earlier ineffective measures that resulted in more American advisors, more American economic aid, and more threats to Hanoi (Logevall, 1999, p. 200).

The United States directed amphibious raids on the North Vietnamese islands of Hon Me and Hon Nieu on July 31 and South Vietnamese forces bombed and strafed a North Vietnamese border post at Nam Can and the village of Noong De on August 1 (Moise, 1996, p. 61). These events served as the immediate backdrop to the Gulf of Tonkin crisis. On August 2 the destroyer USS *Maddox,* at sea to gather electronic intelligence on North Vietnam's coastal defense system as part of a NSA DeSoto mission, was 15 miles from the coast of North Vietnam when its radar detected three approaching North Vietnamese torpedo boats. There is some confusion about what happened next. When key members of the Senate were briefed, they were told that the *Maddox* was 30 miles away from North Vietnam's coastline at the time of the incident, it fired three warning shots at the approaching torpedo boats, and did not resume firing until the approaching boats launched torpedoes. Moise explains that this account is wrong in several ways. He contends that the *Maddox*, trolling dangerously close to the North Vietnamese coastline and fearing a torpedo attack, *initiated* the conflict by firing upon the North Vietnamese torpedo boats once they were within 10,000 yards:

> The *Maddox* had not been thirty miles from the coast, but fifteen, when the torpedo boats were first sighted. The *Maddox* had been trying its best to sink the torpedo boats, and scoring hits with shrapnel from exploding shells if not with the shells themselves, for several minutes before any torpedoes were launched. Finally, when the boats turned away, the *Maddox* pursued and attempted to sink them. (Moise, 1996, p. 88)

Within 15 minutes of the attack, the aircraft carrier USS *Ticonderoga* dispatched U.S. fighter planes that pursued and fired upon the North Vietnamese torpedo boats, leaving four crew members dead and another six wounded (Hanyok, 2005, p. 17).

This incident was minimized in Washington. No American soldiers were wounded and the only damage to the *Maddox* was a single hole made by a machine gun. Johnson did not hold a press conference, issue a public statement, or retaliate. Rather than publicize the clash and risk further criticism from Goldwater, "He instructed his spokesmen to play down the matter, so that the initial Pentagon press release on the subject did not even identify the North Vietnamese as having been involved" (Karnow, 1997, p. 383). The Defense Department described the incident as "unwelcome but not especially serious" (Galloway, 1970, p. 52). Meanwhile, in the Gulf of Tonkin, the U.S. Navy was preparing for war. Just hours after the August 2 attack, the *Maddox*'s Captain, John Herrick, sent Vice Admiral R. B. Moore, the commander of the *Ticonderoga,* the following statement:

> It is apparent that the DRV [Democratic Republic of Vietnam] has thrown down the gauntlet and now considers itself at war with the United States. It is felt that they will attack U.S. forces on sight with

no regard for cost. U.S. ships in the Gulf of Tonkin can no longer assume they will be considered neutrals exercising the right of free transit. (Galloway, 1970, p. 53)

Although he was aware of North Vietnam's willingness to defend its territory, President Johnson did not change course.

On August 3, four U.S.-owned patrol boats attacked a radar installation at Vinh Son and a security post at Cua Ron, both located about 75 miles north of the demilitarized zone separating North and South Vietnam. On the same day, the destroyer *C. Turner Joy* was sent to reinforce the *Maddox* and the aircraft carrier *Constellation* was dispatched to join the *Ticonderoga*. The DeSoto patrols and OPLAN 34A raids continued in the Gulf of Tonkin. At this time, South Vietnam's Prime Minister General Khanh and Ambassador Taylor urged President Johnson to aggressively respond to the August 2 attacks or risk demoralizing his South Vietnamese clients and being viewed by North Vietnam and China as a "paper tiger" (*The Pentagon Papers*, 1971a, p. 189).

The Textbooks Omit August 2

Although the August 2 attack was a significant event that demonstrated the United States' resolve to continue the OPLAN 34A raids as well as North Vietnam's willingness to engage in a military conflict, the textbooks generally avoid the event. Five of the six world history textbooks make no mention of the attack and the one world history textbook that mentions the attack is completely inaccurate. *The Human Experience*, authored by Mounir Farah, an expert on the Middle East, and Andrea Berns Karls, a curriculum specialist, explains, "On August 2, 1964, United States' President Lyndon Johnson announced that North Vietnam had fired on two American destroyers off the coast of Vietnam. Although the incident could not be confirmed, Johnson used it to increase American involvement in the war" (Farah & Karls, 1999, p. 910). This statement is wrong on three counts. First, there was only one destroyer in the Gulf of Tonkin on August 2, the *Maddox*. Second, Johnson never made a public announcement about the August 2 attacks. Third, there has never been any doubt that an attack took place on August 2. It is apparent that Farah and Karls have confused the August 2 incident with the August 4 incident.

The American history textbooks are no better. *Pathways to the Present* and *American Odyssey* make no mention of the August 2 clash. *The Americans* and *The American Vision* also confuse August 2 with August 4. These textbook narratives state, in a nearly identical fashion, "On

August 2, 1964, President Johnson announced that North Vietnamese torpedo boats had attacked *two* American destroyers, the U.S.S. *Maddox* and U.S.S. *Turner Joy*, which were patrolling in the Gulf of Tonkin off the North Vietnamese coast" (Danzer et al., 1998, p. 888, emphasis added). *American Nation* offers a fleeting reference to the August 2 attack. However, it is an indirect reference as it is contained in an extended quote of Johnson's televised speech announcing the alleged attacks of August 4: "The initial attack on the destroyer *Maddox*, on August 2, was repeated today by a number of hostile attacks on two U.S. destroyers with torpedoes" (Boyer, 2005, p. 984). These narratives suggest that the textbook companies and their authors have either (1) ignored the attacks or (2) provided a largely inaccurate representation of what happened in the Gulf of Tonkin in August of 1964.

The August 2 clashes are an important piece of the Gulf of Tonkin puzzle. The August 2 clash, which was a response to the OPLAN 34A raids on North Vietnamese islands, was one event in a protracted covert American war against North Vietnam. This skirmish demonstrated that North Vietnam was willing to engage U.S. forces and that Johnson was determined to continue the DeSoto missions as well as the OPLAN 34A raids *knowing* that it might provoke an international incident. To illustrate this point, on August 3, Michael Forrestal cabled Secretary of State Dean Rusk the following message:

> You probably know that the action against the MADDOX took place within the same 60-hour period as an OPLAN 34A harassing action by SV [South Vietnamese] forces against two islands off the DRV coast. . . . It seems likely that the North Vietnamese and perhaps Chicoms have assumed the destroyer was part of the operation. (*FRUS*, 1964, as cited in Alterman, 2004, p. 211)

This message reveals that although Washington knew that Hanoi perceived the OPLAN 34A raids and DeSoto surveillance missions to be one operation and was willing to engage, the U.S. continued its provocations on August 3.

The Alleged Attacks of August 4

At 9:20 a.m. EST on August 4, U.S. intelligence intercepted North Vietnamese communications suggesting that an attack on the *Maddox* and *C. Turner Joy* was imminent. Later that morning the Pentagon's communications center received a message indicating that the destroyers were being attacked. Before the attack could be confirmed,

Secretary of Defense McNamara approved reprisal attacks from the list of 94 targets drawn up in May and President Johnson decided it was the right time to pursue a congressional resolution that would authorize him to use force in Southeast Asia (Sheehan et al., 1971, pp. 262–263). At 4 p.m., Admiral Sharp informed McNamara that there was some confusion over whether or not the U.S. destroyers were actually attacked. Within the hour McNamara requested the Joint Chiefs of Staff to "marshal the evidence to overcome the lack of a clear and convincing showing that an attack on the destroyers had in fact occurred" (McMaster, 1997, p. 129). At 10:43 p.m., after meeting with congressional leaders, President Johnson ordered Navy fighter-bombers launched from the aircraft carriers *Constellation* and *Ticonderoga*. These bombing missions damaged 25 North Vietnamese patrol boats and 90% of the oil storage tanks near the North Vietnamese city of Vinh (Sheehan et al., 1971, p. 264). Later that night President Johnson made a televised announcement informing the American public, "Repeated acts of violence against the armed forces of the United States must be met not openly with alert defense, but with positive reply. That reply is being given as I speak to you tonight" (Department of State Bulletin, 1964, as cited in Hess, 1997, p. 79).

Although Johnson expressed certainty that an attack took place, American military personnel active in the Gulf of Tonkin on August 4 offered a different version of the crisis. At 7:40 p.m. (Saigon time) on August 4, John Herrick, captain of the *Maddox*, received a message from the National Security Agency (NSA) stating that the North Vietnamese might attack the destroyers again. Later that night, which has been described as a dark, moonless night, punctuated by thunderstorms, the *Maddox*'s radar detected several vessels and its sonar picked up noise spokes resembling incoming torpedoes. Despite the poor visibility, crew members reported seeing cabin lights and torpedo wakes. Aware of the August 2 attacks, as well as the NSA warning, the *Maddox* and *C. Turner Joy* opened fire on spurious radar contacts at approximately 9:40 p.m. Shortly thereafter, Captain Herrick sent a flash cable to Honolulu stating that he was being attacked by North Vietnamese torpedo boats (Alterman, 2004, p. 186). For the next 2 hours, the *Maddox* and *Turner Joy* fired over 300 rounds at "flashing" radar contacts that "appear[ed] on the scope, held for a few sweeps of the radar, then disappeared" (Hanyok, 2005, p. 23).

Later that night Captain Herrick cabled to Washington, "Review of action makes many reported contacts and torpedoes fired appear doubtful. Freak weather effects on radar and overeager sonarmen may have accounted for many reports. No actual visual sightings by

Maddox" (as cited by Drea, 2004, para. 33). This was the first piece of evidence that suggested that there were no attacks on August 4. James Stockdale, a Navy pilot who flew above the *Maddox* and *Turner Joy* for more than an hour and a half on the night of August 4 relates that he "had the best seat in the house to detect boats" and that "no wakes or dark shapes other than those of the destroyers were ever visible to me" (Stockdale & Stockdale, 1984, p. 19). When asked if he saw any boats, Stockdale replied, "Not a one. No boats, no boat wakes, no ricochets off boats, no boat gunfire, no torpedo wakes—nothing but black sea and American firepower" (p. 23).

Likewise, after comparing aircraft movements and reviewing radar contacts, Commander Edmundson (who piloted an A-1 Skyraider dispatched from the *Ticonderoga* to support the destroyers on August 4) concluded that "There were no PT boats, therefore none could be damaged or sunk" (as cited in Moise, 1996, p. 190). In addition to these statements, daylight aerial reconnaissance missions conducted on August 5th failed to find oil slicks or debris from damaged boats that would support the claim that North Vietnamese ships were hit and/or sunk during the attacks (Moise, 1996, p. 202).

A recently declassified NSA article indicates that intelligence officials may have skewed the after-action reports used by Secretary of Defense McNamara and President Johnson. Robert Hanyok, in his analysis of North Vietnamese communications intercepted by U.S. Signal Intelligence (SIGINT), provides four more reasons to doubt that an attack occurred on August 4. First, DRV messages intercepted on August 4 suggest that the North Vietnamese had completely lost track of the destroyers. Second, the boats that the United States claimed attacked the destroyers were actually being recovered after being damaged by American fighters on August 2. Third, a North Vietnam operations review issued on August 6 mentioned the August 2 skirmish and recounted that a U.S. airplane was shot down on August 5, but mentioned no action on August 4 (Hanyok, 2005, pp. 27, 40). Fourth, and perhaps most illuminating, Hanyok's analysis of SIGINT data shows that North Vietnam sent 59 messages between August 3 and 6. Only 6 of the 59 messages were used in the NSA chronology of events pertaining to the Gulf of Tonkin crisis. The six reports used were the only ones that could be interpreted to demonstrate that North Vietnam had aggressive designs. The other 53 reports that were not part of the official chronology

> demonstrated that no attack was planned, or proved that the North
> Vietnamese did not know the location of the American destroyers, or

indicated that salvage operations were the primary activity of Hanoi's navy, or the outright statements in some intercepts for the DRV boats to stay away from the Americans. (Hanyok, 2005, p. 44)

August 4—The Day Textbook Narratives Fail to Question

The historical evidence from the destroyers, pilots, daylight reconnaissance missions, and signal intelligence suggest that no attack took place on August 4. Nonetheless, textbook narratives fail to capture the complexity of this controversial event. In their treatment of August 4, 1964, the textbooks offer three types of accounts. The first type of account simply avoids mentioning August 4. Four of the world history textbooks take this approach. The second type of account offers only Johnson's version of events. This is the line adopted by *A History of the United States* and *World History: Patterns of Interaction.* For instance, *Patterns of Interaction* parrots the official line by stating, "In August 1964, U.S. President Lyndon Johnson told Congress that North Vietnamese boats had attacked two American destroyers in the Gulf of Tonkin" (McDougall Littell, 1999, p. 869). The majority of the American history textbooks also take this approach. *American Odyssey* and *American Vision* uncritically accept Johnson's announcement that "North Vietnamese torpedo boats had attacked two destroyers patrolling the Gulf of Tonkin off the coast of North Vietnam" (Nash, 2002, p. 773).

The third type of account only *implies* that the incident may not have happened. *The Human Experience,* although far from being critical, does qualify Johnson's statement by explaining to students "the incident could not be confirmed" (Farah & Karls, 1999, p. 911). *Pathways to the Present* explains that the details surrounding the August 4 attacks were "sketchy" and that "some people had doubted they had taken place," but fails to elaborate (Cayton et al., 2003, p. 1028). Likewise, *The Americans* uses the word "alleged" to describe the attack, but offers no further explanation (Danzer et al., 1998, p. 888).

The only two textbooks (both written by professional historians, not in-house writers), that come close to challenging Johnson's claims, are *The American Nation* and *A History of the United States.* In a rare critical passage, Boorstin and Kelley explain, "Only later did it turn out that our destroyers might never have been fired upon at all. On a stormy night, they had probably been confused by fake images on the radar screen" (Boorstin & Kelley, 2005, p. 827). Likewise, Boyer explains, "The second attack, moreover, probably never occurred. Some U.S. sailors apparently misinterpreted interference on the radar and sonar as enemy ships and torpedoes" (Boyer, 2005, p. 984).

None of the textbooks, however, offer evidence directly challenging Johnson's problematic, misleading announcement. Although statements from John Herrick, the captain of the *Maddox*, and pilots James Stockdale, Donald Hegrat, and George Edmondson (who categorically denied seeing any North Vietnamese torpedo boats as they flew above the destroyers on August 4), are used in histories of the Gulf of Tonkin crisis, they are not included in any of the textbook narratives. The textbooks also fail to include North Vietnamese response to Johnson's allegations, which they describe as

> an imprudent fabrication inasmuch as in the day and in the night of August 4, 1964, no naval craft of the Democratic Republic of Vietnam were present in the area where the destroyers were allegedly attacked for a second time by North Vietnamese torpedo boats. (Galloway, 1970, p. 501)

Even Johnson expressed doubts about the August 4 attacks, as he later told Undersecretary of State George Ball, "those dumb, stupid sailors were just shooting at flying fish" (as cited in Drea, 2004, para. 6). These statements, in conjunction with statements made by American naval personnel, Moise's examination of the evidence, and Hanyok's analysis of North Vietnam's communications, raise serious questions about an August 4th attack.

THE GULF OF TONKIN RESOLUTION

On August 7, after little deliberation, the Gulf of Tonkin resolution passed by a vote of 88 to 2 in the Senate and 416 to 0 in the House. Framed as a defensive measure, this resolution gave the president the authority "to take all necessary measures to repel any armed attack against the forces of the United States and to prevent further aggression. . . ." (Ellsberg, 2002, p. 16). As mentioned in other accounts, Johnson's ruse worked wonderfully. He was granted the authority to expand the war. In addition, the 58% of Americans who were critical of Johnson's handling of the war prior to the Gulf crisis turned into an 85% approval rating shortly after the incident, putting him in a good position to win the 1964 election in a landslide (Harris, 1973, p. 56).

History has shown that Congress passed the Gulf of Tonkin Resolution without knowledge of Johnson's plans to escalate the war. At the time of its passage, Congress did not know about the OPLAN 34A raids or that the resolution had already been drafted in May 1964 by William Bundy as part of the 30-day plan of political and military machinations designed to create a pretext for direct U.S. attacks on North Vietnam (see earlier description). Greatly concerned about making a favorable case for the resolution, Bundy even prepared detailed responses to awkward questions regarding presidential authority, the scope of permissible actions, and the necessity of a resolution (Barrett, 1997, p. 47). When Johnson brought the resolution to Congress he sent William Fulbright, chairman of the Foreign Relations Committee and Secretary of Defense McNamara, to "dazzle legislators with maps and flip charts" (Karnow, 1997, p. 390).

Congress was also unaware that on August 7, the day the resolution was passed, John McNaughton was drafting a message for Blair Seaborn (who served as Canada's chief delegate to the International Control Commission to oversee the Geneva Agreements) to be delivered to North Vietnam. This message, which was another part of the 30-day escalation plan devised the previous May, instructed Seaborn to inform Hanoi that the nearly unanimous passage of the resolution was an indication that "U.S. public and official patience with North Vietnam is growing extremely thin" and that if Hanoi persisted in intervening in Laos and South Vietnam, "it can expect to suffer the consequences" (Ellsberg, 2002, p. 19). With the exception of the unpopular, and largely ineffectual Senator Wayne Morse of Oregon, who learned about the raids from a Pentagon official, Congress was not informed about the covert war the United States was waging against the DRV for the 6 months leading up to the crisis.

Two Dissenting Votes

Only two members of the United States Senate, Wayne Morse of Oregon and Ernest Gruening of Alaska, voted against the Gulf of Tonkin Resolution. As mentioned, Morse was the only senator who knew about the attacks on North Vietnam. In the Joint Committees session on August 6, Morse expressed his opposition to the resolution:

I am unalterably opposed to this course of action which, in my judgment is an aggressive course of action on the part of the United States. I think we are kidding the world if you try to give the impression that when the South Vietnamese naval boats bombarded two islands a short distance from the coast of North Vietnam we were not implicated.

I think our whole course of action of aid to South Vietnam satisfies the world that those boats did not act in a vacuum as far as the United States was concerned. We knew those boats were going up there, and that naval action was a clear act of aggression against the territory of North Vietnam, and our ships were in Tonkin Bay, in international waters, but nevertheless they were in Tonkin Bay to be interpreted as standing as a cover for naval operations of South Vietnam. (McNamara & VanDeMark, 1995, p. 137)

After Morse delivered these allegations in front of the Joint Committee, McNamara fired back, "[O]ur Navy absolutely played no part in, was not associated with, was not aware of, any South Vietnamese actions, if there were any" (Barrett, 1997, p. 74). In the end, Morse's allegations, which at the time could not be corroborated with evidence, were ignored. The president, the chairman of the Foreign Relations Committee, and the Secretary of Defense secured their resolution by rebuking Morse's claims, taking advantage of patriotic fervor crated by Johnson's televised address, and presenting the resolution as a moderate measure "calculated to prevent the spread of war" (Karnow, 1997, p. 392).

Textbooks Omit Controversy
Surrounding the Gulf of Tonkin Resolution

Morse's assertion of American aggression and the controversy that has come to surround the Gulf of Tonkin Resolution are unwelcome disruptions to the smooth flow of events that textbooks use to represent the United States' decision to escalate the war. The textbook publishers avoid any elements that would disrupt or mar their efforts to establish a patriotic or benevolent imperialist rationale for American involvement. None of the world history textbooks mention any debate about the resolution. Although three of the American history textbooks, *American Odyssey, American Nation,* and *The Americans,* point out that Johnson "Did not reveal that American warships had been helping the South Vietnamese conduct electronic spying and commando raids against North Vietnam," none of them report that Morse vehemently objected to the resolution because of Johnson's failure to inform Congress about the OPLAN 34A raids. Nor do they report that McNamara misled Congress about U.S. sponsorship of the OPLAN 34A raids.

In their efforts to avoid mentioning the Johnson Administration's deceit, the textbooks' authors narrow the discussion to issues of constitutionality. Two of the American history textbooks champion the passage of the resolution by featuring Indiana representative Ross Adair's declaration, "The American flag has been fired upon. We will not and cannot tolerate such things" (Appleby et al., 2005, p. 899; Danzer et al., 1998, p. 888). Two other American history textbooks limit their narratives to an uncritical description of the expansion of presidential authority inherent in the resolution. *America: Pathways to the Present* explains, "The president now had nearly complete control over what the United States did in Vietnam, even without an official declaration of war from Congress" (Cayton et al., 2003, p. 1029). The two textbooks that include Senator Morse, *American Nation* and *A History of the United States,* also limit his opposition to constitutional issues. *American Nation* offers this Senator Morse quote: "I believe that history will record we have made a great mistake. . . . We are giving the President war-making powers in the absence of a declaration of war" (Boyer, 2005, p. 984). None of the textbooks openly discuss Morse's allegations, later proven true, that the United States was waging war against North Vietnam prior to August 1964. This would provide real justification for North Vietnam's concerns and actions, undermine the legitimacy of American military intervention, and call into question the integrity of U.S. actions and policies.

The textbooks also limit Senator Gruening's objections to strictly constitutional issues. In his book *Vietnam Folly* (1968), Gruening argued that the entire Gulf of Tonkin crisis was staged. He pointed out that the Tonkin Resolution was prepared months in advance, that Johnson was using covert raids to escalate the war, and that the *Maddox*'s physical proximity to the OPLAN 34A raids carried out on the North Vietnamese islands of Hon Me and Hon Nieu on the night of July 31-August 1 was "bound to be looked upon by our enemies as an act of provocation" (Gruening & Beaser, 1968, p. 248). Furthermore, none of the textbooks mention that Gruening was especially concerned that the resolution ignored key facts. He believed that it did not acknowledge that the United States was essentially continuing a colonial war initiated by France; that military action was unlikely to bring about peace; and that the corrupt South Vietnamese government did not deserve American economic aid and military support (Johnson, 1998, p. 253).

Despite Morse and Gruening's dissent, the Gulf of Tonkin Resolution passed unanimously in the House, and with only two dissenting voices in the Senate. The resolution passed because the vast majority of Congress could not be convinced what a number of scholars now believe—Johnson was planning to expand the war and that the OPLAN 34A raids and the DeSoto patrols were military provocations.

The Gulf of Tonkin fiasco is a classic example of how an administration determined to go to war can use its monopoly of intelligence information, the authority of the White House, and a compliant media to create a patriotic fervor willing to support war. Indeed, after Johnson made his televised speech announcing that American warships had been attacked in the Gulf of Tonkin, opinion polls revealed that 85% of Americans supported the administration and newspaper editorials echoed this support (Karnow, 1997, p. 391). Rather than offering a lesson to students about how the American public, media, and Congress were once again deceived into supporting military adventures (witness the Mexican-American War, the Spanish-American War, and most recently the Iraq War), textbooks either ignore the controversy surrounding the Gulf of Tonkin or minimize presidential manipulation by focusing on the president's address and the "official" line. By failing to focus on the dissenting voices of members of the military, Congress, and intelligence community, or 40 years of historical scholarship that paints a different picture, the textbooks continue to offer students an inaccurate report of what transpired in the Gulf of Tonkin in the spring and summer of 1964.

CONCLUSION

The textbooks' narratives on the Gulf of Tonkin crisis serve to stifle the development of critical thought by presenting inaccurate, one-sided, patriotic accounts that misrepresent a controversial episode of American history. In their hegemonic distortions, the textbooks fail to mention that the United States was waging a covert war against North Vietnam in the spring and summer of 1964, the alleged attacks of August 4 are now widely known by historians to have been a fabrication, and that the two senators who fiercely opposed Johnson and McNamara's version of what transpired in the Gulf of Tonkin did so because they recognized what was later proven, namely that the president of the United States was deceiving Congress to get a blank check for expanding the war. The textbooks also fail to mention that after the Senate Foreign Relations Committee held hearings in 1968, J. William Fulbright, who helped Johnson garner support for the Gulf of Tonkin Resolution, wrote, "I know I should have been more skeptical. If I had known it was a fraud and a lie in the beginning, I would certainly have acted differently" (Fulbright & Tillman, 1989, p. 106). Even more importantly, in 1995 McNamara himself expressed serious doubts about an August 4 attack (McNamara & VanDeMark, 1995, p. 128). By ignoring key evidence, failing to include alternative perspectives, and reiterating the same falsehoods that were circulated in

August 1964, publishers take a complex, international event and reduce it to historical myth. Will students ever know that President Johnson, who initiated a covert war against North Vietnam in February of 1964, likely used the Gulf of Tonkin incidents as a pretext to expand the war, quiet his presidential opponent, increase his popularity, and appease his faltering South Vietnamese clients?

Having explored the origins of the war and the Gulf of Tonkin crisis in depth, I next turn to another key event of the war, the Tet Offensive. Supporters and critics of the Vietnam War view the Tet Offensive as a major turning point that prompted U.S. withdrawal. Although there is consensus about the importance of Tet, it is the object of much contentious debate, regarding its meaning and role in ending the war and its implications for U.S. foreign policy in general.

CHAPTER 4

Whitewashing the Tet Offensive and the Failures of 1968

On January 31, 1968, North Vietnam and the Vietcong launched a full-scale offensive throughout South Vietnam. The Tet Offensive, timed to coincide with the cease-fires traditionally honored during the lunar New Year, was a coordinated series of attacks on 36 of 44 provincial capitals, 64 district capitals, 5 of South Vietnam's major cities, 50 hamlets, Saigon's airport, the Presidential Palace, and the American Embassy (Herring, 2002b, pp. 228–229). Color television brought the Tet Offensive into American homes as reporters captured images of a Vietcong unit attacking the U.S. Embassy, the North Vietnamese siege on the ancient city of Hue, the 6,000 marines surrounded by 30,000 North Vietnamese soldiers at Khe Sanh, and perhaps most memorably, South Vietnam General Nguyen Ngoc Loan's street execution of Vietcong captain Nguyen Van Lem. Just as the Gulf of Tonkin incidents represent a major turning point in the U.S. escalation of the Vietnam War, the Tet Offensive represents a major turning point; it pushed the Johnson Administration toward a negotiated settlement. In what follows, I investigate how textbooks represent the intelligence failure that led to Tet, the media's coverage of the war, the decline of American morale, and the My Lai and My Khe massacres.

THE INTELLIGENCE FAILURE

Throughout 1967, Military Assistance Command, Vietnam (MACV) interpreted the Order of Battle (estimates of enemy strength) to indicate that the United States was winning the war of attrition. In July, total enemy forces were estimated to be 297,790. (The total number of enemy forces includes five groups: maneuver troops, combat support personnel, administrative service, irregulars, and political cadres.) By December 31, new estimates suggested a significant decrease in enemy strength as total enemy forces were reduced to 224,581 (Wirtz, 1991a, p. 244). The Pentagon's Order of Battle Estimates, although disputed by the CIA, suggested that the "crossover point" had been reached. Johnson's top military advisors, as well as General Westmoreland, believed that enemy losses exceeded the rate at which the Vietcong could replenish their army through recruitment and North Vietnamese infiltration (Wirtz, 1991a, p. 245).

In addition to information suggesting the enemy was weakening, American commanders believed that South Vietnam's rural population would not participate in a massive uprising. Wirtz (1991a) explains that

> U.S. commanders and analysts had many sources of information about the Southern population, not the least of which were the contacts with their ARVN [Army of the Republic of Vietnam] counterparts, and this accurate information indicated that the South Vietnamese population would not revolt in support of the communists. (p. 127)

Believing that there was little support for a mass urban rebellion, reports of such a strategy were dismissed by American intelligence personnel as communist propaganda. Or, as one army officer who participated in the intelligence analysis said after the attacks, "If we'd gotten the whole battle plan, it wouldn't have been believed. It wouldn't have been credible to us" (as cited in Oberdorfer, 1971, p. 121).

Indeed, General Westmoreland's annual report for 1967 suggested the United States was making progress. Westmoreland wrote, "the enemy had lost control of large sectors of the population" and now "faces significant problems in areas of indigenous recruiting, morale, health and resources control" (*The Pentagon Papers*, 1971b, p. 538). Westmoreland went on to state that the year closed with "the enemy increasingly resorting to desperation tactics in attempting to achieve military/psychological victory; and he has experienced only failure in these attempts" (*The Pentagon Papers*, 1971b, p. 538). Just days before the lunar New Year, estimates of enemy strength, reports of South Vietnamese indifference to joining a mass rebellion, and Westmoreland's optimistic assessment made a major Vietcong offensive against South Vietnam's population centers appear improbable, if not suicidal.

The Khe Sanh–Dienbienphu Analogy

American assumptions about the enemy was a second factor diverting the military planners' attention away from Tet. In the fall of 1967, General Westmoreland and President Johnson believed that North Vietnam's General Vo Nguyen Giap was interested in replicating the French loss at Dienbienphu. Both fully understood the symbolic value of this battle. In 1954, French General Henri Navarre assembled 12,000 elite forces in a failed attempt to lure the Vietminh, led by General Giap, into a battle at Dienbienphu, a remote village located in Northwestern Vietnam. After less than 2 months of heavy fighting, and with the international community watching, the Vietminh routed the French forces, effectively ending French involvement in Vietnam. This time, the United States would be surrounded at Khe Sanh, a heavily guarded military fortress located in the mountains of South Vietnam's Northwestern region.

In addition to understanding the symbolic importance of losing a major battle, Westmoreland had many reasons to believe the Vietcong and North Vietnamese were planning a major assault on Khe Sanh. On January 2, 1968, American troops spotted just outside of Khe Sanh a group of six high-ranking North Vietnamese officers, including a regimental commander. Two days later, two North Vietnamese regiments were reported to have moved into the mountains southeast of Khe Sanh. On January 20, a defector appeared east of the U.S. base and explained that the North Vietnamese intended Khe Sanh to be a replay of Dienbienphu and that attacks would begin that night (Oberdorfer, 1971). Indeed, on the night of January 21-22, communist troops began shelling a U.S. outpost at Khe Sanh. In response to these developments, Westmoreland contacted Washington stating, "I believe that the enemy sees a similarity between our base at Khe Sanh and Dienbienphu and hopes, by following a pattern of activity similar to that used against the French, to gain similar military and political ends" (Wirtz, 1991a, p. 205). In his estimation, Giap's primary objective was taking Khe Sanh:

In view of American and South Vietnamese strength, for the VC [Vietcong] and North Vietnamese to emerge from hiding throughout the country would be to invite catastrophic losses and certain defeat. The large enemy build-up in the DMZ [demilitarized zone] and at Khe Sanh an established fact, it would be much more logical and promising for him to stage diversionary attacks elsewhere while concentrating on creating something like a Dienbienphu at Khe Sanh and seizing the two northern provinces. (Westmoreland, 1976, p. 316)

Westmoreland fell for the diversion. He diverted military reserves away from the population centers to reinforce Khe Sanh and the DMZ. He also convinced President Johnson that the impending assault on Khe Sanh would be a repeat of the battle for Dienbienphu that had occurred 14 years earlier. Shortly before the Tet Offensive, Johnson required each of his generals to sign a formal agreement stating that the fortress would be held (Hess, 1997).

Missing the Signals

Westmoreland's belief in American progress and insistence that a decisive battle would be fought at Khe Sanh compelled him to misread the many signals suggesting an impending Vietcong North Vietnamese offensive against South Vietnam's cities. In September 1967, North Vietnam's General Vo Nguyen Giap wrote an essay entitled, "Big Victory, Great Task." Giap explained that American forces would be drawn to the border areas by a feint, thus leaving South Vietnam's cities unprotected. He stated, "The political struggle of our urban compatriots in the South will play an increasingly important role and we will hit the enemy directly in his deepest lairs" (Giap, 1967, p. 301). U.S. intelligence experts dismissed Giap's essay as propaganda because it contradicted American reports suggesting that the enemy was not capable of staging such an attack, and that the South Vietnamese people would not support a rebellion.

As General Westmoreland, President Johnson (who monitored developments at Khe Sanh on a sand table erected in the White House), and the American press become fixated with daily reports of Khe Sanh, evidence of a major attack in South Vietnam continued to pile up. Throughout the latter half of 1967, the CIA detected a significant increase in truck traffic along the Ho Chi Minh Trail. In the fall of 1967, the Army of the Republic of Vietnam (ARVN) acquired a document dated September 1 delineating a three-pronged offensive designed to rout ARVN, destroy U.S. military installations, and incite mass rebellion in the cities. In January 1968, 42 weapons caches had been found in and around South Vietnam's Dinh Tuong province. Shortly after, the Associated Press published an intercepted document calling for Vietcong troops to "flood the lowlands . . . move toward liberating the capital city . . . take power and try to rally enemy brigades and regiments to our side one by one" (Oberdorfer, 1971, p. 119).

Although Westmoreland dismissed these signals as propaganda, American intelligence and military officers expressed concern about an impending attack in South Vietnam. Joseph Hovey, Robert Layton, and James Ogle, CIA intelligence specialists stationed in Saigon, wrote a formal report predicting a Vietcong/North Vietnamese attempt to lure American forces away from the cities, attack urban targets, incite mass rebellion, and force American withdrawal. On January 10, General Fred Weyand explained to General Westmoreland that there was some weak but alarming intelligence suggesting that the enemy was going to make a move toward the population centers, including Saigon.

Despite the mounting evidence and American reports of an impending attack on South Vietnam's cities, General Westmoreland and President Johnson continued their preoccupation with Khe Sanh. On the eve of the Tet Offensive, half of the ARVN soldiers charged with protecting South Vietnam's cities were granted holiday leave, 200 U.S. colonels celebrated at a pool party in Saigon, and President Johnson received hourly reports and closely monitored Khe Sanh. Meanwhile, the North Vietnamese and Vietcong were making their final preparations for an offensive that would reach into the southernmost zones of South Vietnam.

On January 30, 1968, President Johnson held his regularly scheduled foreign affairs luncheon. Among those in attendance were Secretary of State Dean Rusk, Secretary of Defense McNamara, CIA Director Helms, and General Wheeler. After opening the meeting, Johnson asked General Wheeler for an update on Khe Sanh. General Wheeler responded, "At Khe Sanh the situation is quiet and the weather is good. At 9:00 a.m. today EST General Westmoreland said that he had talked with his commander at Khe Sanh and the situation is well in hand" (Barrett, 1997, p. 577). Only moments later, W. W. Rostow, Johnson's National Security Advisor, interrupted the meeting by announcing, "We have just been informed we are being heavily mortared in Saigon. The Presidential Palace, our BOQs [Bachelor Office Quarters], the Embassy and the city itself have been hit." President Johnson responded, "This could be very bad" (p. 578).

On January 30, 1968, the Vietcong and North Vietnamese initiated a sweeping offensive that extended from the demilitarized zone that separated North and South Vietnam to the southern tip of South Vietnam, located some 400 miles away. In the first 2 weeks of the offensive, the United States lost 1,100 soldiers, the ARVN lost 2,300 soldiers, an estimated 12,500 South Vietnamese civilians were killed, and another 1,000,000 became refugees (Herring, 2002b, p. 232).

The Lessons of Tet

For the North Vietnamese and the Vietcong, the Tet Offensive was both a defeat and a victory. On the one hand, Tet represented a conventional military defeat. It did not cause a mass rebellion and 37,000 Vietcong soldiers were killed. On the other hand, given the Johnson Administration's optimistic reports, the death of 1,100 American forces in a few weeks of fighting was high. And when viewed as a guerilla war, the Vietcong *did* achieve many objectives. Andrew Krepinevich, a U.S. Army Major and foreign policy expert, relates that these achievements included derailing the U.S. pacification effort, shocking the American public, demonstrating that populated areas were not safe from insurgent attacks, increasing South Vietnam's refugee population, and furthering South Vietnam's economic woes (Krepinevich, 1986, p. 249). Tet also influenced senior policymakers back in Washington. It demonstrated that the United States could not win a limited war in Vietnam and prompted key officials like Clark Clifford, McGeorge Bundy, and Dean Acheson to abandon escalation. Historian David F. Schmitz argues that the most important outcome of the Tet Offensive was that it resulted in "a crackling of elite consensus" and changed the views of the establishment (Schmitz, 2005, pp. 165–166).

While Tet may have represented a limited strategic victory for the resistance, it also represented a massive intelligence failure for the United States. Historians, journalists, and military officials have consistently pointed out that General Westmoreland, preoccupied with what he thought was going to be a major offensive at Khe Sanh, underestimated the numerous signs that an attack was going to take place throughout South Vietnam. A military history textbook issued to West Point cadets in 1969, the year after Tet, stated, "The first thing to know about Giap's Tet Offensive is that it was an Allied intelligence failure ranking with Pearl Harbor in 1941 or the Ardennes Offensive in 1944" (Palmer, 1978, p. 179). Journalist Neil Sheehan explained that Khe Sanh was "the biggest lure of the war. The Vietnamese Communists had no intention of staging a second Dienbienphu there. The objective of the siege was William Westmoreland, not the marine garrison" (Sheehan, 1988, p. 710). In a similar fashion, military writer Dave Palmer (1978) relates that after Tet, "General Giap was satisfied with his handiwork. He never had any intention of capturing Khe Sanh. His purpose there all along had been to divert Westmoreland's attention and resources. Khe Sanh was a feint, a diversionary effort. And it had accomplished its purpose magnificently" (Palmer, 1978, p. 172).

In the broader sense, the intelligence failure that led to the Tet Offensive highlights the United States' inability to estimate enemy strength as well as predict its next move. This is a theme that is apparent throughout the histories of the war. Halberstam's *The Best and the Brightest* (1969) described Kennedy and Johnson's top policymakers as men who suffered from delusions of American omnipotence and who had little understanding of Vietnam or the powers of nationalism. Historians and Vietnamese experts have written extensively about how these failures to understand Vietnam resulted in ineffective policies, prolonged the war, and eventually led the United States to abandon their South Vietnamese clients (Fitzgerald, 1972; Hackworth & Sherman, 1989; Herring, 2002b; Kahin, 1979; Krepinevich, 1986; McNamara & VanDeMark, 1995; Sheehan, 1988).

HISTORY TEXTBOOKS
AND THE INTELLIGENCE FAILURE THAT WASN'T

Although historians, journalists, and military officials have labeled the Tet Offensive a massive intelligence failure, textbooks do not include any such commentary. None of the world history or American history textbooks make any reference to the intelligence failures that preceded Tet. The world history textbook *Patterns of Interaction* does not even mention the Tet Offensive. The other five world history textbooks explain, in nearly identical fashion, that Tet was the Vietnamese New Year, the communists launched a major attack, American and South Vietnamese forces repelled the attack, and that the television coverage led Americans to oppose U.S. involvement. To illustrate, Ellis and Esler, writing for Pearson-Prentice Hall, describe the Tet Offensive in the following terms:

> In 1968, guerilla forces launched a massive attack on American and South Vietnamese forces. The assault was unexpected because it took place at Tet, the Vietnamese New Year. Although the communists did

not capture any cities, the Tet Offensive marked a turning point in public opinion in the United States. It also showed that the North Vietnamese would fight at any cost. (Ellis & Esler, 2005, p. 874)

This description is almost identical to that offered by Holt, Rhinehart, and Winston:

At the beginning of 1968, North Vietnam launched a major attack called the Tet Offensive, named for the Vietnamese New Year on which it began. Although American and South Vietnamese forces drove the Communists back, many Americans who saw the fierce fighting on television began to openly oppose U.S. involvement in the War. (Holt, Rhinehart, & Winston, 2005, p. 867)

Three of the American history textbooks, *The American Nation, The American Vision,* and *Pathways to the Present,* describe the Tet Offensive in similar terms, although with more detail. The other three American history textbooks, *A History of the United States, The American Odyssey,* and *The Americans* take up a slightly more critical position, pointing out that the large-scale attack contradicted Westmoreland's optimistic reports of American progress. Boorstin and Kelley explain:

In 1968, General William Westmoreland, the American commander in Vietnam, issued another optimistic report telling how the war was being won. Four days later, on the Vietnamese New Year holiday called "Tet," the Viet Cong and North Vietnamese suddenly launched their strongest offensive. . . . General Westmoreland claimed correctly that the Tet episode was actually a victory for the United States and South Vietnam. The Communists had suffered enormous losses. It would take them years to rebuild their strength. But the Communists had seized the offensive, and in this, the first war shown on TV, the American public had witnessed the horrors. (Boorstin & Kelley, 2005, p. 813)

None of the textbooks, however, mention that in the days leading up to Tet, General Westmoreland was repeatedly made aware of captured documents and reports suggesting that a large-scale attack on South Vietnam's population centers was imminent. Furthermore, the textbooks do not make any mention of Khe Sanh. Yet the Khe Sanh diversion is included in orthodox, revisionist, and critical histories of the Vietnam War (Herring, 2002b; Krepinevich, 1986; Lewy, 1978; Lomperis, 1984; Schmitz, 2005; Young, 1991). Stanley Karnow's Pulitzer-Prize winning *Vietnam: A History* (1997) offers a four-page description of the relationship between Khe Sanh and the Tet Offensive. He describes Khe Sanh as a ruse "intended to draw Americans away from South Vietnam's population centers, thereby leaving them naked to assault" (Karnow, 1997, p. 554). Although there is historical consensus that Tet was linked to Giap's Khe Sanh diversion, textbooks completely avoid mentioning this U.S. military failure.

By focusing on the nature of the attack and the disproportionate casualties, the textbooks make a massive intelligence failure out to be a conventional military victory, albeit with political repercussions. Depicting the Tet Offensive in such a way omits Westmoreland's failures and simultaneously precludes students from learning about the complexity of collecting, interpreting, and analyzing intelligence data. The intelligence failure should not be offered to merely discredit or pass judgment on American military officials (however instructive that might be) or to underscore Giap's successful ploy. Rather, like the major histories of the Vietnam War, it should be done in the spirit of educating students about the mind-set of military and political leaders that failed accurately to interpret intelligence reports that suggested an impending attack. Narratives that demonstrate how intelligence gathering works, when it has been successful (as was the case of thwarting the attack on Los Angeles' U.S. Bank Tower in 2002), and the repercussions of intelligence failures (such as Pearl Harbor, Tet, 9/11, and Iraq) offer students meaningful learning opportunities about the mind-sets that allow political and military leaders to fall victim to delusions of American power.

PUBLIC OPINION AND THE TET OFFENSIVE

The United States' effort to win the hearts and minds of South Vietnam was coming undone before the Tet Offensive of 1968. During 1967, more than 200 U.S. soldiers were being killed and 1,400 wounded each week (Spector, 1993, p. 9). In September 1967, President Johnson implemented a tax surcharge to cover the $1 billion that the United States was spending each month. In addition to these signs of failure, a Department of Defense report named the Jason study (after a division of the Department of Defense) was released in December 1967. Commissioned by McNamara and headed by Jerome Wiesner of MIT and George Kistiakowsky of Harvard, the team of 49 natural and formal scientists concluded "As of October 1967, the U.S. bombing of North Vietnam has had no measurable effect on Hanoi's ability to mount and support military operations in the South" (*The Pentagon Papers*, 1971b, p. 223).

If the situation in Southeast Asia was not bad enough, things were also deteriorating at home. On November 1, the Secretary of Defense released a report calling for a halt to the bombing of North Vietnam, limiting additional troop deployments, and transferring military operations to South Vietnamese forces. Of particular concern to McNamara was the fact that "the American public, frustrated by the slow rate of progress, fearing continued escalation, and doubting that all approaches to peace have been sincerely probed, does not have the appearance of having the will to persist" (McNamara, 1995, p. 308). Indeed, throughout 1967 influential Americans such as Dr. Martin Luther King Jr., Senators William Fulbright and Robert Kennedy, columnist Walter Lippmann, as well as pediatrician Dr. Benjamin Spock, publicly expressed opposition to the war.

McNamara was right. By 1967 the American public was losing the little faith it had in the U.S. war effort. When asked if they believed the United States made a mistake in entering the fighting in Vietnam, 47% of Americans responded "yes" in October 1967, just 4 months before the Tet Offensive. This was nearly twice the number of people who responded "yes" when the question was first asked in August 1965 (see Figure 4.1). Likewise, Johnson's job approval ratings declined significantly *prior to* the Tet Offensive. In January of 1966, 57% of Americans approved of the way Johnson was handling the Vietnam War. This approval rating plummeted to 32% in August of 1967, some four months before the Tet Offensive (see Figure 4.2).

A similar pattern can be detected by examining shifting opinions in 1967. In February 1967, 44% of Americans thought the U.S. military progress was improving. By August of the same year, public support dwindled, as 63% of Americans believed that "Our side was *not* doing better" (Harris, 1973, p. 60, emphasis added). Without question, disillusion and discontent with the Vietnam War emerged *prior to* the Tet Offensive. In fact, the Vietnam War was never a popular war with the American public. As early as November 1963, only 32% of Americans believed Vietnam was worth fighting a full-scale war for, and 37% of the American public indicated it would rather lose Vietnam than wage a full-scale war in Southeast Asia (Harris, 1973, p. 55). Presidents Kennedy and Johnson only received full public support during critical moments like Diem's assassination, the Gulf of Tonkin crisis, the initiation of Operation Rolling Thunder, and when Johnson elected to bomb areas around Hanoi and Haiphong. This support was short-lived. For instance, whereas 58% of the American public supported Johnson's handling of Vietnam before the Gulf of Tonkin crisis, 85% of the public supported Johnson after the incident. Four months later,

FIGURE 4.1. Percentage of Americans Responding "Yes" When Asked If They Believed the U.S. Made a Mistake Entering the War in Vietnam (by month/year)

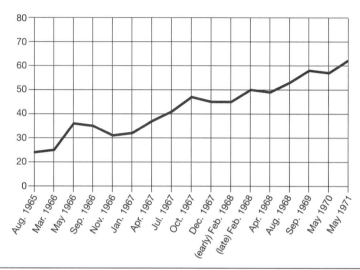

Source: Adapted from Roper, 1977, p. 698

FIGURE 4.2. Percentage of Americans Who Approved of Johnson's Handling of the War in Vietnam (by month/year)

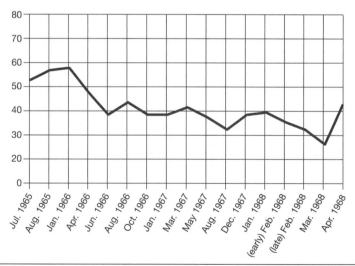

Source: Adapted from Roper, 1977, p. 700

only 38% of Americans supported Johnson's handling of the war. The Harris poll summarizes this rally around the flag effect: "Only specific crises have galvanized the American people to full and united support of government action in Vietnam. Overall, there remains a sense of frustration and uneasiness" (Harris, 1973, p. 57).

HOW THE MEDIA "SABOTAGED" THE WAR

Despite public opinion poll data indicating that the American public did not fully support the Vietnam War before the Tet Offensive (or for any amount of time during the entire war) General Westmoreland blamed the media for turning public opinion against the war effort. He explained "the general tone of the press and the television was critical, particularly during the Tet Offensive" (Westmoreland, 1976, p. 421). In one sense, Westmoreland was right. In perhaps the best analysis of the media's coverage of the Vietnam War, Hallin (1986) explains that prior to Tet, "editorial comments by television journalists ran nearly four to one in favor of administration policy; after Tet, two to one against" (p. 161). Furthermore, military historian William Hammond explains that within hours of the attack, the media ran pessimistic stories expressing doubts about American progress in Vietnam. Mike Wallace of CBS News commented that Tet "demolished the myth" that the U.S. and ARVN controlled South Vietnam (Hammond, 1988, p. 345). In February 1968, returning from a fact-finding mission to Vietnam, Walter Cronkite declared,

> To say that we are closer to victory today is to believe, in the face of the evidence, the optimists who have been wrong in the past. To suggest we are on the edge of defeat is to yield to unreasonable pessimism. To say that we are mired in a stalemate seems the only realistic, yet unsatisfactory conclusion. (Cronkite, 1996, pp. 257–258)

Following Westmoreland, revisionist historians also adopt this stab-in-the-back thesis, treating the media as a subversive agent that turned public opinion against the war, forcing American withdrawal (Gelb & Betts, 1979; Hanson, 2001; Lewy, 1978; Podhoretz, 1982). Likewise, textbook narratives adopt the revisionist "stab-in-the-back" thesis. Consider these statements:

> Although American and South Vietnamese forces drove the Communists back, many Americans who saw the fighting on television *began*

to openly oppose U.S. involvement in the war. (Holt, Rinehart, & Winston, 2005, p. 867, emphasis added)

Many Americans had been confident that victory in Vietnam was in sight, but the Tet Offensive showed that such optimism was uncalled-for. Many Americans *began* to openly oppose involvement in the war. (Holt, Rhinehart, & Winston, 1999, p. 762, emphasis added)

As images of the fighting flooded American television, many people at home *began* to express reservations about American involvement in Vietnam. (Cayton et al., 2003, p. 1036, emphasis added)

The political effect of the offensive was stunning. It *shook* U.S. confidence by revealing that no part of South Vietnam was secure—not even downtown Saigon. (Boyer, 2005, p. 993, emphasis added)

Tet also marked a turning point in the war. It showed that no place in Vietnam—not even the American embassy—was safe from attack. It *shattered* American confidence and *raised* grave doubts about Johnson's policies in Vietnam. (Nash, 2002, p. 777, emphasis added)

The mainstream media, which reported the war in a skeptical but generally balanced way, *now* openly criticized the war. (Danzer et al., 1998, p. 902, emphasis added)

Public opinion *no longer* favored the president. In the weeks following the Tet offensive, the president's approval rating plummeted to a dismal 35%, while support for his handling of the war fell even lower, to 26%. (Appleby et al., 2005, p. 907, emphasis added)

These textbooks treat Tet as the effective beginning of public dissatisfaction or as a media spectacle that undermined American confidence. This assertion is wrong in two ways. First, as mentioned above, public opinion surveys indicate that the American public was never fully behind the Vietnam War. Therefore, there was little confidence to undermine. Second, it is difficult to measure how much impact the media's coverage of the Tet offensive and its aftermath had on public opinion. Rather than a crisis or turning point, Tet marked a sharp decline in public opinion on a larger slope of eroding public opinion. "When viewed in the larger perspective of the entire war," Roper suggests, "Tet appears to have been 'one more incident,' one that reminded the public that the war was not going well . . . and that helped move public opinion along in the anti-war direction it had been moving for nearly three years" (Roper, 1977, p. 703). Or, in Clarence Wyatt's words:

> It's incorrect to blame—or credit—either Tet or the press coverage of it with creating a great turn in public or press opinion. The Tet Offensive was the war in microcosm—superior American firepower against superior North Vietnamese political will. Similarly, press coverage of the offensive, and the relationship between the press and the government in those weeks, reflected the way the press approached the story and the way it related to the government throughout the war. Tet was less the occasion of a sudden shift in such opinion than it was a confirmation of characteristics and trends that had been around a long time. (1993, p. 182)

By depicting the media as a subversive element, students are deprived of the opportunity to engage in complex historical analysis by weighing the evidence and forming their own opinions about the media's role in the war. Indeed, there is also evidence suggesting that even after the Tet Offensive the media continued to support the war. In February 1968, the *Boston Globe* examined the editorial stances of 39 leading newspapers representing a combined circulation of approximately 22 million papers. The study revealed that not a single major American newspaper suggested the United States withdraw from Vietnam (Cohen, 2001).

The media's role in the Vietnam War will continue to be a topic of debate. Rather than embracing historical complexity, textbooks adopt the revisionist stab-in-the-back thesis, precluding teachers and students from actively examining the relationship between the press and government in times of war. Textbooks also divert students' attention away, recognizing that by 1968, the United States' war effort was coming undone, the antiwar movement had moved into the mainstream, and the government was running a deficit to pay for this failing war. Thus, students are relieved of grappling with the notion that for 5 more years Johnson and then Nixon prosecuted an expensive, deadly war without strong public support or a formal declaration of war.

TET AND THE DECLINE OF AMERICAN MILITARY MORALE

Although American forces crushed the initial stage of the general offensive by March 1968, the second and third waves of attacks, although not as lethal as the first, were launched in May and August. These 3 waves of attacks were responsible for the bloodiest year in the Vietnam War; 16,589 U.S. soldiers were killed in 1968 alone. Not only was 1968 the deadliest year, but it was also a year marred by racial conflict, widespread drug abuse, and the military cover-up of the massacres at My Lai and My Khe. In this final section, I explore how textbooks represent the other historical developments of 1968.

Racial Tension Among U.S. Forces in Vietnam, 1968

Although Vietnam is often considered the first fully integrated American war, 1968 marked an increase in racial tensions for soldiers serving in Vietnam. Throughout the war, there was a great deal of conflict over discrimination in promotions and field assignments. The visibility of Confederate flags on uniforms, military vehicles, and even military barracks was another source of conflict. After arriving in Vietnam in January 1968, Eddie Kitchen, an African American lieutenant, was appalled by the highly visible Confederate flags. In a letter to his mother, Kitchen wrote,

> We are fighting and dying in a war that is not very popular in the first place and we still have some stupid people who are fighting the Civil War. . . . Black soldiers should not have to serve under the Confederate flag or with it. We are serving under the American flag and the American flag only. (as cited in Spector, 1993, p. 245)

American military police were also a source of friction as African Americans believed that the military police, who were mostly white, regularly discriminated against African American soldiers by routine stops, searches, and an "overzealous enforcement of rules that did not apply to whites" (Spector, 1993, p. 246). Racially charged violence also increased in Vietnam between 1968 and 1969. In the period between October 1968 and September 30, 1969, "a pattern of black subject and white victim was found in 19.2% of all murders, 50% of cases of attempted murder, 43% of aggravated assault, and 71% of cases of robbery" (Lewy, 1978, p. 155). In the same time frame, African Americans comprised 58% of the stockade population, even though they represented only 9.1% of the U.S. troops fighting in Vietnam (p. 155). Although these numbers do not necessarily mean that each crime was racially motivated, they do suggest that racial tension existed and that blacks represented a disproportionate number of incarcerated soldiers.

On September 30, 1968, *Newsweek* reported a race riot at the army stockade at Long Binh. Angry about unequal treatment and discrimination, some 250 African American soldiers overpowered their prison guards, unlocked the gates, and set fire to the administration and other buildings. After Military Police (MP) reinforcements arrived, a melee broke out between the MPs and the African American prisoners. *Newsweek* reported that after order was restored, 220 uncooperative prisoners, all of whom were African American, with the exception of three Puerto Ricans, "proceeded to shed their uniforms and to don white kerchiefs and African-style robes which they made out of Army blankets" (Stokes, 1968, p. 35).

By 1969, soldiers began segregating themselves. Writing for *Time* magazine, Wallace Terry reported that Black troops had organized "Ju Ju" and "Mau Mau" groups to protect themselves against racial prejudice and intimidation. In their efforts to assert their political power and cultural identity, African American soldiers registered their complaints collectively, wore amulets that symbolized Black pride, displayed flags adorned with spears and Black faces, and devised Black Power handshakes. Revealing his awareness that inequalities at home were reproduced in Vietnam, one African American Marine commented, "Why should I come over here when some of the South Vietnamese live better than my people in 'the world'? We have enough problems fighting white people back home" (Terry, 1968, p. 705).

Drug Abuse by U.S. Forces in Vietnam, 1968

In addition to racial tensions, the U.S. military was also marred by an increase in drug usage. By the time of the Tet Offensive, a growing number of soldiers had used marijuana before entering the military and the production of marijuana and heroin had become a major industry in Southeast Asia. A Pentagon study revealed that the possession and use of marijuana by U.S. soldiers had increased 260% from 1967 to 1968 (Spector, 1993, p. 274). A similar study conducted by Dr. Wilfred Postal and Dr. E. Caspar found that about 30–35% of American soldiers admitted to smoking marijuana while in Vietnam (p. 275). This was the beginning of what would prove to be a serious military problem. In 1970, the U.S. military estimated that up to 65,000 soldiers were using drugs and that approximately 40,000 were addicted to heroin (Herring, 2002b, p. 301). By 1971, a Department of Defense study found that 50.9% of the army had smoked marijuana, 28.5% had used narcotics such as heroin and opium, and 30.8% had tried other psychedelic drugs (Lewy, 1978, p. 154). One helicopter pilot described just how pervasive drug abuse was in Vietnam:

> The majority of people were high all the time. . . . For ten dollars you could get a vial of pure heroin the size of a cigarette butt, and you could get liquid opium, speed, acid, anything you wanted. You could trade a box of Tide for a carton of prepacked, prerolled marijuana cigarettes soaked in opium. (as cited in Karnow, 1997, p. 646)

By 1970, drug abuse assumed epidemic proportions. Between the spring and fall of 1970, the number of drug overdoses had increased from an average of two deaths per month to two deaths per day (Spector, 1993, p. 277). In addition, 1968 marked the beginning of violence against commanding officers. Between 1969 and 1971, 630 incidents of "fragging" (using fragmentation grenades to intimidate, injure, or kill a commanding officer), were reported (Lewy, 1978, p. 156). One study of 800 separate fragging incidents found that each perpetrator reported using a wide variety of drugs and "87.5% reported being acutely intoxicated at the time of the incident" (as cited in Sorley, 1999, p. 292). Writing in 1971, Marine Colonel Robert Heinl asserted that

> our army that now remains in Vietnam is in a state approaching collapse, with individual units avoiding or having refused combat, murdering their officers and noncommissioned officers, drug ridden, and dispirited where not near-mutinous. (as cited in Young, 1991, p. 256)

Textbook Treatment of American Morale in 1968

In their treatment of the deteriorating American military situation in 1968, the textbooks cut away from Vietnam after the first wave of the Tet Offensive in January and February. The world history textbooks do not devote any space to capturing what was happening in Vietnam during and after the Tet Offensive. The entire sample of world history textbooks are remarkably similar in that the narratives move directly from the Tet Offensive to Johnson's decision not to run for reelection, Nixon's policy of Vietnamization, and then to the 1973 Paris Accords that resulted in a cease-fire and eventual American withdrawal. Students studying the Vietnam War in their world history classes will not read about the problems faced by the U.S. military during and after the Tet Offensive.

None of the American history textbooks make any reference to the problems that plagued the U.S. military after the first stage of the Tet Offensive. When textbooks do take up the issue of race relations and drug abuse, these issues are disconnected from 1968 and the Tet Offensive, as they are located in previous sections devoted to describing the ground war from 1965 to 1967. In their treatments of race relations, *The American Vision* and *The American Nation* point out that African Americans made up a disproportionate number of military deaths. "In 1965, for example, African Americans accounted for almost 24 percent of all battle deaths, even though they made up just 11 percent of the U.S. population" (Boyer, 2005, p. 985). Both textbooks, however fail to include any information regarding the racial tension during 1968 and later. *A History of the United States, Pathways to the Present*, and *American Odyssey* do not broach the subject of race relations or disproportionate deaths. *The Americans*, coauthored by Louis E. Wilson, the chair of the African Studies Department at Smith College, is the only history textbook that directly mentions racial tensions. He provides students with the following passage:

> Many African Americans experienced the same racism in Vietnam that they endured at home. Throughout the war, racial tensions between white and black soldiers ran high in many platoons. In some cases the hostility led to violence. In 1967 [*sic*], a race riot erupted at the U.S. army stockade at Long Binh Vietnam. Two years later, black and white marines returning from war clashed at Camp Lejeune, North Carolina. The racism that gripped many military units was yet another factor that led to low troop morale in Vietnam. (Danzer et al., 1998, p. 897)

The Americans is the only textbook to make the connection between the racism experienced in the United States and the racism that existed during the Vietnam War. Nonetheless, the text inaccurately mentions one race riot (the Long Binh riot took place in August 1968, not 1967, and was not the only race riot in Vietnam), without offering the context of the problem, examples of racism experienced by African American soldiers, or details that illuminate the pervasive nature of racial tension in the U.S. and in Vietnam.

The American history textbooks also minimize drug abuse. Four of the textbooks altogether avoid the issue. *The American Odyssey* and *The Americans* are the only textbooks that make any reference to the drug abuse problem. After listing the challenges of fighting in a guerilla war and encountering mines, booby traps, ambushes, and hit-and-run raids, Nash minimizes the severity of the problem by asserting,

"Some turned to drugs to escape" (Nash, 2002, p. 775). Although failing to provide specific statistics attesting to the extent of drug abuse in Vietnam, *The Americans* does a much better job representing the problem. Danzer et al. informs students that as the war progressed and morale declined, "Many soldiers turned to alcohol, marijuana, and other drugs to deal with the futility of a war that seemed less and less winnable" (Danzer et al., 1998, p. 893). In this one sentence, *The Americans* accomplishes more at capturing the reality of troop morale and drug abuse than all the other major textbooks.

1968—THE YEAR OF THE MASSACRES AT MY LAI AND MY KHE

As the Tet Offensive marked a rise in American casualties, racial tensions, and drug abuse, it also marked an increase in animosity toward Vietnamese people. By the time the first wave of Tet attacks had been quelled in February 1968, American soldiers had become increasingly frustrated with a war that had come to be viewed as "essentially purposeless and aimless" and that frustration was increasingly directed at the Vietnamese people, both North and South, soldier and civilian (O'Brien, 1998, p. 177). In the following section, I examine how one of the most controversial events of the war, the My Lai massacre, is presented in textbooks.

The Massacres at My Lai and My Khe

At approximately 7:30 a.m. on March 16, 1968, a barrage of artillery shells were fired into the hamlet of My Lai as villagers were preparing their breakfasts. Shortly after the village was shelled, U.S. Charlie Company landed by helicopter outside My Lai, surrounded the hamlet, and began firing at unarmed civilians, killing livestock, and burning homes. The killing continued for 4 hours as Colonel Frank Barker, Colonel Oran Henderson, and Major General Samuel Koster hovered above in helicopters witnessing the atrocities. In an act of bravery, helicopter pilot Hugh Thompson, furious at what he saw on the ground, intervened by airlifting two old men, two women, and five children to safety. By 12:00 p.m., 504 Vietnamese civilians had been killed (some raped and then killed) in My Lai and the neighboring hamlet of My Khe. Not a single bullet had been fired at American troops. Michael Bernhardt summarized the day's operation: "We had no casualties. It was just like any other Vietnamese village—old papasans, women, and kids. As a matter of fact, I don't remember seeing one military-age male in the whole place dead or alive" (as cited in Hersh, 1970, p. 76).

In an official report of the incident, Colonel Oran Henderson stated that

> approximately twenty noncombatants had been inadvertently killed by preparatory fires and in crossfire between friendly and enemy forces, and that the reports of unnecessary killing civilians was merely another instance of a command Viet Cong propaganda technique and were useless. (as cited in Hersh, 1970, p. 97)

The official line was that there was no massacre, only a small number of unintended civilian casualties.

The American public did not learn about what transpired in My Lai and My Khe for 20 months. The crime was covered up until helicopter pilot Ron Ridenhour wrote President Nixon, the Pentagon, and several influential members of Congress describing civilian executions, heaps of dead bodies, and the point-blank execution of a young boy who "just stood there with big eyes staring around like he didn't understand" (Ridenhour, 1969, p. 202). The American public learned about the My Lai massacre when Seymour Hersh published a series of articles in the *New York Times* in September 1969. Military photographer Ron Haeberle's photographs of the civilian bodies piled in a drainage ditch reinforced these stories.

A military inquiry was not initiated until November 1969. Completed in March 14, 1970, the Peers Report found that U.S. Army troops of Task Force Barker "massacred a larger number of noncombatants in two hamlets of Son My village" and that in the ensuing months, "At every command level within the American Division, actions were taken, both wittingly and unwittingly, which effectively suppressed information concerning the war crimes committed at Son My village" (Anderson, 1998, pp. 207–210). In April 1971, a military court-martial found U.S. Army Lieutenant William Calley guilty of murdering 22 Vietnamese civilians and sentenced him to lifetime imprisonment. President Nixon intervened, and after several appeals, Lieutenant Calley served only 4½ months in Fort Leavenworth (Anderson, 1998, p. 12). He was the only soldier ever to be punished. None of his commanding officers were convicted. Captain Ernest L. Medina, who gave the order, "Kill everyone, leave no one standing," was represented by F. Lee Bailey and found not guilty of murdering civilians. No senior officials who planned the operation, witnessed it, or covered up the atrocities were convicted of any crimes. This incident was one incident in a larger pattern of violence resulting in the indiscriminate murder of Vietnamese civilians, both directly by soldiers as well as by aerial campaigns—as journalists, historians, and veterans have documented (Herr, 1978; Kerry, 1991; Schell, 1988; Young, 1991; Zinn, 1967).

Westmoreland's War of Attrition

The My Lai massacre was the by-product of General Westmoreland's war of attrition, where dead Vietnamese bodies served as a barometer of military progress. Unlike previous wars, progress was not measured by winning territory. In Vietnam, the number of enemies killed measured progress. James Gibson points out that "Producing a high body count was crucial for promotion in the officer corps" (Gibson, 1986, p. 112). In the 9th infantry division, a 1 to 50 ratio of "allied to enemy dead" was the mark of a "highly skilled unit," whereas a 1 to 15 ratio was "Low but acceptable for a U.S. unit" (p. 113).

In an effort to destroy the enemy, the U.S. military used saturation bombing, the application of over 100 million pounds of chemical herbicides, the establishment of free-fire zones, and search-and-destroy missions. This framework, combined with inherent racism, pressure, drugs, military training, and the inability to distinguish friend from foe, offers an explanation about why so many civilians were killed. Philip Caputo, an author and journalist who served in the Vietnam War as an infantry lieutenant in the U.S. Marines, described the practical consequences of General Westmoreland's war of attrition:

> General Westmoreland's strategy of attrition . . . had an important effect on our behavior. Our mission was not to win terrain or seize positions, but simply to kill: to kill Communists and to kill as many of them as possible. Stack 'em like cordwood. Victory was a high body count, defeat a low kill-ratio, war a matter of arithmetic. The pressure on unit commanders to produce enemy corpses was intense, and they in turn communicated it to their troops. This led to such practices as counting civilians as Viet Cong. "If it's dead and Vietnamese, it's VC," was a rule of thumb in the bush. It is not surprising, therefore, that some men acquired a contempt for human life and a predilection for taking it. (Caputo, 1977, p. xix)

At least, in theory, these military tactics and weapons would lead to a "crossover" point when enemy losses outpaced the rate at which soldiers could be replaced (Hess, 1997, pp. 94–96). Westmoreland believed that once this had been achieved, the Vietcong and the North Vietnamese would be forced to abandon their resistance to superior U.S. firepower.

When combined with the day-to-day rigors of fighting against an unseen enemy, the policy of attrition allowed, if not spurred, civilian abuses. In the weeks before the My Lai massacre, Charlie Company sustained a number of losses to ambushes, mines, and booby traps they believed were planted by women and children. This stress of fighting an unseen enemy was directed at civilians. Charlie Company's Ron Grzesik described the increasing pattern of violence:

> It was like going from one step to another. First you'd stop the people, question them, and let them go. Second, you'd stop the people, beat up an old man, and let them go. Third, you'd stop the people, beat up an old man, and then shoot him. Fourth, you go in and wipe out a village. (as cited in Hersh, 1970, p. 43)

In the days leading up to the massacre, Charlie Company had looted villages, intimidated, tortured, raped, and executed civilians, and lied about their conduct in official reports.

Textbook Cover-Up of the My Lai Massacre

Although world history textbooks make space for the Amritsar Massacre in India that resulted in the deaths of some 400 protesters who fought against British colonial rule, none of them devote a single sentence to the 504 civilians killed at My Lai and My Khe.

The American history textbooks' treatment of the My Lai massacre is inconsistent. None of the textbooks include the massacre at My Khe, where an estimated 100 civilians were also killed on March 16, 1968, as part of a larger search-and-destroy mission of the village of Son My, of which My Lai and My Khe were but two hamlets.* Boyer's *The American Nation*, which mentions the U.S. use of cluster bombs, agent orange, napalm, and the 500,000 South Vietnamese civilians that were killed, makes no reference to the My Lai massacre.

The other five American history textbooks provide a justification for civilian deaths. These textbooks rationalize the U.S. war of attrition as a necessary, albeit deadly, measure to contain communism

---

*When a symposium of writers, scholars, veterans, and former military officers convened at Tulane University in 1994, they accepted 504 as the best estimate of civilian deaths in the two hamlets of Son My Village (Anderson, 1998, p. 4).

in Southeast Asia. Two of these textbooks (written by different publishers and authors) include nearly identical anecdotes describing a Vietnamese woman selling soft drinks who might be a Vietcong ally and a child on the corner waiting to throw a grenade at America soldiers (Cayton et al., 2003, p. 1031; Danzer et al., 1998, p. 891). Faced with a treacherous jungle terrain, losing public support, scrutinized by the international community, and fighting the resolute Vietcong who used guerilla tactics, attacking and retreating into the jungle, hiding among civilians, planting booby traps, and constructing elaborate tunnel systems, the unfettered application of American firepower was the logical solution to the problem of Vietnamese resistance.

Other textbooks take a relativistic tit-for-tat approach, suggesting that American atrocities were no worse than those perpetrated by the Vietcong and North Vietnamese. *A History of the United States* and *Pathways to the Present* preface their descriptions of the My Lai massacre by pointing out the Vietcong were responsible for massacring civilians during the Battle for Hue, just a few weeks prior to My Lai. In a section entitled "Communist Brutality," which directly precedes the section entitled "Massacre at My Lai," *Pathways* asserts that "some 3,000 to 5,000 were killed" by communist forces who were "uncommonly brutal, slaughtering anyone they labeled an enemy, including minor officials, teachers, and doctors" (Cayton, et al., 2003, p. 1035). Neither of those textbooks that preface My Lai with the massacre at Hue informs students that independent sources never confirmed the actual number of civilians killed and there has been much debate about how many of the civilian deaths in Hue were the product of communist "brutality"; how many were civilians killed during 3 weeks of intense American bombing, shelling, and strafing; and how many were enlisted soldiers (many were wearing military uniforms) killed in combat (Porter, 1974).

Only two of the six textbooks, *The Americans* and *Pathways to the Present*, inform students that there was a cover-up. For example, *The Americans* explains, "Twenty-five officers were charged with involvement in the massacre and subsequent cover-up, but only Calley was convicted and imprisoned" (Danzer et al., 1998, p. 908). None of the textbooks let students know that high-ranking military officers observed the massacre from helicopter, listened to radio transmissions, and falsified reports describing what transpired (Hersh, 1972). Nor do textbooks mention that Ridenhour and Hersh had great difficulty finding an American newspaper that would run the story and it broke in the United States only after it made the papers in England and Germany (Anderson, 1998, p. 55).

What textbooks do offer students are narratives that dehumanize the victims and decontextualize the event. For instance, three of the six American history textbooks offer Private Paul Meadlo's testimony about his role in the massacre:

> We huddled them up. We made them squat down. . . . I poured about four clips [about 68 shots] into the group. . . . Well, we kept right on firing . . . I still dream about it. . . . Some nights, I can't even sleep. I just lay there awake thinking about it. (Cayton et al., 2003, p. 1035)

While Meadlo's testimony describes the event, it also serves to conceal the context and aftermath of the crime, and fails to show that it was not an aberration but part of a systematic campaign of destruction wrought by saturation bombing, search-and-destroy missions, use of chemical herbicides, and free-fire zones. This quote describes one event, only from a soldier's perspective, and thus fails to capture the full tragic nature of the event and the brutalities of war. Testimonies of Vietnamese people who survived the massacre are not included. These textbooks do not reveal how the atrocity destroyed families and shattered the lives of those who managed to survive the ordeal. For example, Truong Thi Le, who lost nine members of her family on March 16, 1968, expressed bitter resentment more than 20 years after the incident:

> I think of it all the time and that is why I am old before my time. I remember it all the time. I think about it and I can't sleep. I'm all alone and life is hard and there's no one I can turn to for help. Then I think of it all the time. I'm always sad and unhappy and that's why I'm old.
>
> I think of my daughter and my mother, both of them dead. I think of it and feel extremely bad.
>
> I won't forgive. I hate them very much. I won't forgive them as long as I live. Think of those children, that small . . . those children still at their mothers' breasts being killed. . . . I hate them very much. . . .
>
> I miss my mother, my sister, my children. I think of them lying dead. I think of it and feel my insides being cut to pieces. (Bilton & Sim, 1992, p. 23)

Students do not read about how the massacre ruined the lives of so many Vietnamese civilians. None of the textbooks include military photographer Ron Haeberle's photographs of dead civilians lying in a drainage ditch. To include this evidence would complicate the historical narrative undermining the myth of war. In the end, textbook narratives that fail to include any of the victims' names, photographs, or testimonies completely dehumanize the My Lai villagers.

By largely omitting the larger pattern of destruction and civilian abuse experienced by the people of Quang Ngai Province (where the hamlets of My Lai and My Khe were located), the textbook narratives effectively cover up the atrocities against civilians. For instance, after flying reconnaissance missions of Quang Ngai Province in 1967, Jonathon Schell estimated that between 1965 and 1967, "the Marines, the Army, the Korean Marines, and the ARVN had destroyed seventy percent of the villages in the province, which means seventy percent of the houses" (Schell, 1988, p. 198). Schell also relates that a British physician working in Quang Ngai's only civilian hospital estimated 50,000 Vietnamese civilians were injured or killed each year in Quang Ngai alone (p. 395).

In addition to minimizing American misdeeds during the Vietnam War and avoiding controversy that could impugn the United States (and risk stirring up controversy during the adoption process), all of the textbooks also fail to inform students that after Congress refused to investigate American war crimes, Vietnam veterans held a series of "Winter Soldier" investigations "for the purpose of exposing war crimes committed by American forces and their allies in Vietnam" (Stacewicz, 1997, p. 232). On the first day of the Detroit investigation, Bill Crandell, a former platoon leader, announced, "We intend to demonstrate that My Lai was no unusual occurrence. . . . We intend to show that the policies of the American division which inevitably resulted in the My Lai massacre were the policies of other Army and Marine divisions as well" (Brinkley, 2004, p. 347). Students are not permitted to read John Kerry's 1971 congressional testimony delineating American violations of the Geneva Conventions by "the use of free-fire zones, harassment interdiction fire, search-and-destroy missions, the bombings, the torture of prisoners, [and] the murder of prisoners" (Kerry, 1991, p. 156).

CONCLUSION

The nation's leading social studies textbooks avoid controversy by offering patriotic descriptions of the Tet Offensive and the conditions of the military in 1968. Instead of depicting the Tet Offensive as a massive intelligence failure, the narratives avoid any mention of Khe Sanh and limit the Tet Offensive to a surprise attack by a cunning adversary. Although the Vietnam War was never a popular war and the anti-war movement moved into the mainstream in 1967, most of the textbooks adopt the conservative stab-in-the-back thesis suggesting that the media's coverage of Tet was a critical event turning the American public against the war. With few exceptions, the textbook narratives largely gloss over the racial strife, drug abuse, and overall decline in military morale that coincided with the Tet Offensive. Only 5 of the 12 textbooks mention the My Lai massacre. When it is mentioned, several textbooks ignore or minimize the cover-up, dehumanize the victims, and treat the massacre as an isolated event in a war "where most American soldiers acted responsibly and honorably" (Appleby et al., 2005, p. 911).

CHAPTER 5

Recovering Democratic History Education in an Era of Standardization

The 12 textbooks I've been following in this study omit controversial aspects of the Vietnam War. Although the United States devised and directed the OPLAN 34A raids, textbooks represent them as South Vietnamese raids only supported by the United States. Despite the fact that a number of historians, intelligence experts, elected officials, and military officers offer compelling evidence that there was no August 4 attack on American ships, all 12 textbooks failed to include these voices. Whereas powerful political leaders like William Fulbright and Robert McNamara eventually expressed doubts about the evidence used to support the passage of the Tonkin Gulf Resolution, the textbooks did not touch upon these developments. Likewise, all 12 textbooks omitted any reference to the Khe Sanh diversion and the intelligence failure that preceded Tet. Although key public opinion polls show that public disenchantment began before January 1968, several of the textbooks suggested that the media's coverage of the war is what subverted public support. And perhaps the most invidious of misrepresentations, the majority of textbooks treat the My Lai massacre as an aberration. Although there are some minor exceptions, this recent crop of widely distributed textbooks whitewashes the Vietnam War by offering uncritical, hegemonic accounts of the Gulf of Tonkin crisis and the Tet Offensive. To use Vietnam historian Christian Appy's expression, the memory of the Vietnam War has been "muffled" (Appy, 1999, B4).

THE MYTH OF WAR

Muffling the controversial aspects of the Vietnam War comes as no surprise when we consider that the corporate production process is designed to purge content that may be considered objectionable. By limiting the historical narrative to minor issues of tactics, strategy, and policy, but avoiding larger questions concerning the legitimacy of the war, government deception, and the moral dimensions of military action, textbooks also resonate with perhaps the most enduring and widely promoted of American historical myths: the myth of war. Mosse (1990), in his study of public memory of the World Wars, explains that the myth of war emerged alongside the development of nation-states in the 18th century.

> The myth of war experience was designed to mask war and to legitimize the war experience; it was meant to displace the reality of war. The memory of war was fashioned into a sacred experience which provided the nation with a new depth of religious feeling, putting at its disposal ever-present saints and martyrs, places of worship, and a heritage to emulate. (p. 7)

Tangible symbols such as war memorials, park monuments, poetry, national anthems describing military heroism, and days of remembrance were created to legitimize war-making, honor the fallen soldier, and make war a sacred event that would appeal to future generations.

The myth of war serves two functions. By conflating war-making with the security of the state and the protection of the citizenry, the myth of war serves to quell opposition or even reasoned debate. In his famous funeral oration dedicated to Athenian soldiers killed in the opening battles of the Peloponnesian War, Pericles (431 BC) equated military service with preserving Athenian freedom, love for country, and heroism. As the bodies of Athenian soldiers were reduced to ashes, Pericles counseled grieving families to fix their eyes on the greatness of Athens: "And when this power of the city seem great to you, consider that the same was purchased by valiant men, and by men that knew their duty . . ." (Thucydides, 1629/1989, p. 113). Roughly 2,300 years later, Abraham Lincoln made similar appeals to allay the lingering hostilities of the Civil War. Looking out on the battlefield at Gettysburg, Lincoln suggested that military sacrifice furthered the United States' experiment in democracy:

> that from these honored dead we take increased devotion to that cause for which they gave the last full measure of devotion—that we here highly resolve that these dead shall not have died in vain . . . that this nation, under God, shall have a new birth of freedom—and that government of the people, by the people, for the people, shall not perish from the earth. (Lincoln, 1863, para. 3)

Both Pericles and Lincoln fully understood the power of language to sanctify the war experience and forge bonds between the living and dead (Wills, 1992). By conflating war-making with the preservation of state, war transcends rational discourse, and to question war is an act of betrayal, or a stab in the back tantamount to treason. Baker (2006) describes how right-wing ideologues have deployed the stabbed-in-the-back thesis to limit rational discourse on military operations and censure those who speak against unmitigated war. In the wake of the Chinese Communist Party's victory and the Soviet Union's detonation of an atomic bomb in 1949, Republicans led by Senator Robert Taft censured President Franklin Roosevelt for appeasing Stalin at the Yalta Conference of 1945. Roosevelt's willingness to negotiate a postwar peace (which both Republicans and Democrats initially supported in 1945) is viewed as an act of betrayal that effectively surrendered Eastern Europe to the Soviets and emboldened communist leaders. Blame has also been pinned on President Truman for General MacArthur's defeat in Korea in 1950. Never mind the questions surrounding MacArthur's strategy to send American troops north directly into Chinese forces in the dead of winter. Truman, who denied MacArthur's request to drop some 30 atomic bombs on the Chinese region of Manchuria, is held responsible for the U.S.-Korean stalemate.

And so it is with Vietnam. Although the United States dropped more bombs on Southeast Asia than in all theaters of World War II combined, revisionists blame Johnson and McNamara for failing to use maximum military force against North Vietnam. The domestic antiwar movement is blamed for losing the war in Vietnam (Lomperis, 1984; Podhoretz, 1982). In an effort to portray those who opposed the Vietnam war as alien, un-American, and communists, Nixon's vice president Spiro Agnew, Pentagon officials, and influential members of the political Right created the myth that Vietnam Veterans were spat on upon returning home. This myth served as powerful symbol of betrayal, dissuading mainstream Americans from joining the antiwar movement (Lembcke, 1998).

By calling our attention to battlefield heroics while diverting it away from the brutality of combat, the myth of war also functions to preserve war as a viable, even appealing, foreign policy option. For instance, the best-known photograph of World War II, Joe Rosenthal's Raising the Flag on Iwo Jima, taken on February 23, 1945, portrays one Navy medic and five U.S. Marines struggling to raise the U.S. flag over Mount Suribachi during the battle of Iwo Jima. This bloodless image of American servicemen struggling together to raise the American flag serves as an archetype for the myth of war: It simultaneously draws the viewers' attention to supreme acts of heroism and service to nation, while diverting attention away from the human costs of war (some 6,800 Americans soldiers were killed during the monthlong battle for Iwo Jima and 29,700 Japanese soldiers were killed attempting to defend the island).

This powerful symbol of national sacrifice, however, is only loosely based on what happened on Mount Suribachi on February 23. It was not taken under enemy fire, as it suggests. Rather, it was taken after an initial Marine patrol reached the top of Mount Suribachi, secured the area, and raised a smaller flag. It was taken without incident as photographers, military officers, and marines looked on. Nevertheless, this photograph was awarded the Pulitzer Prize and was later the basis for Felix de Weldon's massive 40-foot bronze sculpture located in Washington, D.C. The Truman administration seized upon this powerful symbol of sacrifice and courage to promote the war effort and preserve the myth. It was printed on some 137 million postage stamps, used as the official advertisement of the 1945 bond drive, and featured in numerous Marine recruiting posters (Marling & Wetenhall, 1991).

Taking a broader view, Andrew Woods Jr. (2008), a veteran severely wounded in the liberation of France, contends that our memories of World War II are largely mythical memories. He explains that popular memoirs, film, and literature have purified our memory of World War II as a "good war" won by the "greatest generation" of Americans. Remembering World War II in this manner requires a historical amnesia that disregards the countless civilians killed (he estimates between 50 and 60 million) by both the Axis and Allies, minimizes the psychological trauma experienced by returning soldiers, and discounts the devastating losses of human life and property incurred by our French and

British allies (Woods, 2008). Woods explains that for many Americans, these myths promote industrial war and the concomitant killing of civilians as a legitimate, if not desirable, means to vanquish evil and the forces of darkness. These myths, he explains, are partially responsible for public acceptance of the United States leading the world in military spending, the development and stockpiling of weapons of mass destruction, and the manufacturing and export of conventional arms.

Today the myth of war is very much alive and has been used to win and maintain public support for the wars in Afghanistan and Iraq. The Bush administration resurrected the myth of war to build consensus for the war in Iraq. In August 2002, Vice President Cheney made a speech to Veterans of Foreign Wars in which he inflated Iraq's weapons capabilities. Cheney declared, "There is no doubt that Saddam Hussein now has weapons of mass destruction. There is no doubt he is amassing them to use against our friends, against our allies, and against us" (Cheney, 2002, as cited in Daalder & Lindsay, 2003, p. 157). Six months later, Bush opened his State of the Union Address with the warning, "The gravest threat facing America and the world, is outlaw regimes that seek and possess nuclear, chemical, and biological weapons" (Bush, 2003, as cited in Cirincione et al., 2004, p. 76). On March 19, 2003, the United States, without the support of key members of the U.N. Security Council, launched a preemptive invasion of Iraq. No weapons of mass destruction were ever found. No connection to Al-Qaeda was ever established.

The media has actively maintained and promoted the myth of wars in Iraq and Afghanistan. In its attempts to control the press's coverage of the wars, the Pentagon requires reporters to agree to follow the "ground rules" for reporting from the battlefield (Katovsky & Carlson, 2003, p. 408). Public misinformation campaigns have been used to make heroes out of ordinary soldiers like Jessica Lynch and cover up friendly fire deaths of high-profile servicemen like former NFL player and Army Ranger Pat Tillman (Associated Press, 2008). From 1991–2009, the American press was precluded from taking photographs of the caskets shrouded in American flags that move through Dover air force base to soldiers' final resting places. Even honoring servicemen by mentioning the names of the dead is taboo. For example, when Ted Koppel decided to honor the 700 dead American servicemen by reading their names on an April 30, 2004 episode of *Dateline*, Sinclair Corporation (which owns 62 television stations in 39 markets) pulled the episode. Sinclair Vice President for Corporate Relations Mark Hyman expressed concern that Nightline anchor Ted Koppel "is opposed to the war and is trying to stir up public opposition to it" (Public Broadcasting Services, 2004, para. 3).

Wrapped in the flag, the myth of war manipulates our nationalism and love for country. It treats war as the foremost option for self-preservation and the most powerful means of vanquishing our enemies. It relies on the uncritical acceptance of official pronouncements and mindless dependence on the corporate media to dehumanize our declared foes and instill a blind sense of patriotism that stifles deliberation and debate. The myth of war draws upon false choices to force the citizenry into passively accepting American military operations. You are either with us or against us. Questioning the preemptive invasion and open-ended occupation of Iraq is giving aid and comfort to our terrorist enemies. By agreeing to "support the troops," we are compelled to abandon our ethical and moral responsibilities and quietly endure armed conflict regardless of the human cost. Pulitzer Prize–winning *New York Times* war correspondent Christopher Hedges puts it best:

> War as a myth begins with patriotism, which always begins with thinly veiled self-glorification. We exalt ourselves, our goodness, our decency, our humanity, and in that self-exaltation we denigrate the other. War as myth allows us to suspend judgment and personal morality for the contagion of the crowd. War means we do not face death alone. We face it as a group. And death is easier to bear because of this. We jettison all moral precepts we have about the murder of innocent civilians, including children, and dismiss atrocities of war as the regrettable cost of battle. (Hedges, 2003, para. 6)

The myth of war's pervasiveness and potency leads to one very big question: "What do we, as teachers, do to create classroom environments that allow and even encourage students to think critically about past, present, and future American wars?" My answer to this question is simple: let's set aside standards-based learning initiatives, compromised textbooks, and high-stakes exams, and return to our democratic tradition of education that views learning as a continual process where students actively engage in authentic inquiry, exploring the past, and constructing knowledge.

RECOVERING DEMOCRATIC EDUCATION

In Plato's *Allegory of the Cave*, Socrates asks Glaucon to imagine a fictitious situation in which a group of prisoners has been confined in an underground cave since childhood. Behind the prisoners burns a fire, and between it and the prisoners is a path along which free people carry artifacts, casting shadows on the wall which prisoners are forced to look at. Having no choice but to look at the shadows of the free people and their artifacts, Socrates suggests "the shadows of artefacts . . . constitute the only reality people in this situation would recognize" (Plato, 1993, p. 241). Continuing with the allegory, Socrates asks Glaucon to imagine that one of the prisoners was unchained and dragged into the light, forced to see the source of the shadows, as well as the sun, moon, and stars. With this new vantage point, the liberated prisoner discovers the sources of the shadows, and the limitations imposed by the confinements of the cave. Pushing further, Socrates asks Glaucon, What if the liberated prisoner was forced to return to the darkness of the cave? Would he struggle to make sense of, and appreciate the menagerie of shadows that his fellow prisoners accept as real? And perhaps more importantly, how would the prisoners respond to him? Would his fellow prisoners, working from such limited experience, find his new worldview corrupted and reject his new knowledge? Glaucon's response: "They certainly would" (p. 243).

Originally written to rationalize the rule of philosopher kings, Plato's *Allegory of the Cave* offers a series of metaphors that capture the contradictions of history education in an era of standard-based learning dominated by corporate interests. As teachers, state and federal laws compel us to reduce history education to a ritual of superficial coverage of predetermined curricular objectives. Faced with hundreds of curricular objectives and measured by standardized exam scores, teachers have little choice but to choose one point of reference, of a small number of corporate textbooks, as the primary source of historical information. This study shows, however, that textbook narratives that largely downplay controversy, ignore key evidence, and mute critical voices effectively reinforce the myth of war. These hegemonic narratives make poor substitutes for authentic historical inquiry, where teachers lead students in freely exploring the historical record, interpreting the past, and deliberating the implications for today. Faced with these curricular constraints, the past is grossly distorted. Thus, we are presented with a dilemma. As history educators, do we resign ourselves to conjuring shadows of the past to be mastered by our students in compulsory settings? Or, do we work toward a pedagogical approach that provides students with the knowledge and skills to grapple with the complex nature of historical inquiry and a richer understanding of war-making? And if we do, what does this type of work look like and how can we communicate a more democratic, empowering form of history education to our students and our colleagues?

Given the problematic nature of textbook narratives and the standardization of teaching and learning, it is imperative that teachers take it upon themselves to offer students opportunities to actively study history, critically examine their textbooks, and develop skills that will allow them to effectively participate in governing their nation. Critically examining war requires teachers to take risks by stepping out of the maze of objectives and engage in what is widely known by history educators as "historical thinking." Historical thinking treats history as a production subject to political influence that can be, and often is, used to stymie critical thought and socialize students into accepting the written word as Truth. Rather than passively accept that which is transmitted in curricula and textbooks, Wineburg argues that students must attend to authors' hidden assumptions, or subtexts, and view historical narrative as a human construction, not official, uncontested truth. He explains that teachers are called to "attend to the human motive in the texts we read; called on to mine truth from the quicksand of innuendo, half-truth, and falsehood that engulfs us every day; called on to brave the fact that certainty, at least in understanding the social world, remains elusive and beyond our grasp" (Wineburg, 2001, p. 83). This form of instructional practice stands in contrast to standards-based education in important ways:

- Historical thinking assumes that students are sentient beings who possess the capacity to construct knowledge by asking questions, finding and evaluating evidence, analyzing issues, and forming conclusions.
- There is no one source of historical knowledge; rather, students are trained to move beyond textbook narratives and examine a panoply of sources representing different perspectives, cultural assumptions, and worldviews.
- Historical study cannot be value-free, objective, or neutral. Experience and values shape the way we understand, interpret, and represent the past. Attending to these dimensions of historical thinking offers important opportunities to learn about the social, political, and economic forces that shape the world.
- Authentic historical inquiry treats knowledge as tentative, tolerates ambiguity, and leaves itself open to new information, interpretations, and ways of thinking.

As history educators charged with preparing students for active citizenship, we must lead our students into engaging the past as a resource for understanding their lives and for acting upon the future. Dewey, the most ardent and articulate advocate for democratic education, explains

> the purpose of school education is to ensure the continuance of education by organizing the powers that insure growth. The inclination to learn from life itself and to make the conditions of life such that all will learn in the process of living is the finest product of schooling. (1966, p. 51)

The difference between Dewey's education for democracy and the present technical system of standardized curricula and tests is a fundamental assumption about the ends of education. The present system is designed to impart bits of knowledge that can be measured on paper-and-pencil exams. For most students, learning history ends with the completion of the final exam. To be educated is a technical act aimed at mastering a predetermined, fixed body of value-free information. Macedo (1994) explains that this type of education, which fragments knowledge and seals off learning from the larger sociopolitical structures of a society, creates semiliterates who read the *word* but lack the capacity to read the *world*.

Democratic education embraces the many ways of knowing and rejects final answers or "unassailable truths" to be mastered and measured on paper-and-pencil exams. The past cannot be mastered—it is too complex, multidimensional, and the very attempt to master some false sense of "the past" is a political act that obstructs our understanding of those aspects of the past deemed unworthy of mastery. Rather than merely working to support students in understanding discrete pieces of the past, democratic education concerns itself with instilling the habits, temperament, and skills that support students in critically examining the social, political, and economic forces that shaped the past (reading the world) as preparation for continuously working to improve the future, both personally and collectively.

The point here is not to subvert the system of standardized curricula and exams; rather, the point is to transcend the artificial parameters the state imposes on teaching and learning by introducing students to their own intellectual powers and teaching them how to employ those powers to direct their lives. Plato explains that education should not be concerned with introducing knowledge into empty minds like introducing sight into eyes that are blind. Instead of "imparting sight into the organ," Plato suggests education "should proceed on the understanding that the organ already has the capacity, but is improperly aligned, and isn't facing the right way" (Plato, 1993, p. 246). In this sense, democratic education is not concerned with "mastering" a preordained body of information, but building personal knowledge through active inquiry and the application of reason. As more information becomes available, new questions emerge, interpretations continuously change, the discourse shifts, and knowledge grows. Doing history in this manner illuminates the tentative nature of knowing and leaves students with more questions than answers. Each student will apply a new set of experiences and a unique way of knowing to the study of history. Authentic forms of assessment will require students to defend their thoughts with logic and reason. The end result is the development of a critical awareness where students ask questions, search for answers, and form their own working understandings of the world.

To accomplish this, teachers must resist the state's demands to regiment teaching and learning and work to make classrooms public spaces that minimize corporate interests. History educators interested in empowering students to think historically will rightly acknowledge the role deliberation, disagreement, and values play in historical interpretation and argument. Rather than seeking to impart the right interpretation and arriving at historical truth, democratic teachers engage in a dialogue about the past. By entering into a dialogue with students, teachers become advocates for free education rather than agents of socialization and/or indoctrination. Noddings (2002) explains that an education that values students' experiences and abilities resists quantifiable methods of measurement: "The participants do not know at the outset what the conclusions will be. Both speak; both listen" (p. 16). Indeed, the wisest Athenian citizens were those who were aware of the limits of their knowledge, but nonetheless tirelessly pursued expanding those boundaries through questioning, critical reflection, and dialogue.

BEYOND THE STANDARDIZED CURRICULUM AND CORPORATE TEXTBOOK

If we are serious about students achieving a fuller understanding of war, teachers must reach beyond textbooks and lead students in directly exploring the historical record. Textbook narratives that focus on official pronouncements, minimize controversy, and marginalize the perspectives of declared enemies, render war as a manageable, and even appealing, foreign policy option. These textbook messages, by themselves, may appear trivial and perhaps even meaningless.

However, these messages do not stand alone. Textbook narratives resonate with messages transmitted in the mainstream media, echoed in the halls of government, and reified in the virtual worlds of video games. Students have been socialized into accepting these messages even before they enter the classroom. Textbooks reinforce what students have already been told. Repeating these messages in compulsory settings, where standards-based learning evaluates the degree to which students accept and restate these statements, is an act of political socialization. Rather than assisting students in grappling with the historical complexity, history education and classroom teaching becomes an act of socializing students into accepting one (of many) interpretations of the past. The interpretations offered in these textbooks reinforce the myth of war and in doing so prepare students to accept, even support and defend, this myth.

In this final section I offer a heuristic designed to have students think critically about war. I use the term "heuristic" as it implies a process of investigation and self-discovery, supported by critical thought, careful deliberation, and robust debate—the hallmarks of democratic education.

This heuristic provides teachers and students with the intellectual tools to engage in historical inquiry. The underlying assumption is that history education should support students in accessing and engaging the issues of the world, not serve as a barrier to serious encounters with the past. This work is not simply doing history for the sake of knowing the past; rather, it is to provide students with the tools to think clearly about war, evaluate motives and policies, and explore the multitude of ways human beings experience military conflict. This heuristic is not a simple list of exercises that can be completed in allotted blocks of time. It is an approach that requires teachers and students to explore new avenues of inquiry in making meaning of military conflict and pursuing knowledge. There is no prescribed or fixed end at which students will be delivered and a test administered. Rather, the objective is to complicate the study of war, and have students ask hard questions of the historical record.

This heuristic consists of six core concepts: (1) war is an act of human agency; (2) international law provides a basis to study acts of war; (3) the media plays an important role in building consensus for war; (4) voices of opposition offer opportunities to learn about war; (5) the government uses political language to stifle debate; and (6) corporate textbooks promote the myth of war. By requiring students to work directly with the historical record, each of these concepts provide students with opportunities for authentic historical inquiry.

War Is an Act of Human Agency

Too often war is treated as an omnipotent force that operates independently. Textbooks treat the Vietnam War with statements like, "The War Escalates"; "The War Unfolds"; and "Going to War in Vietnam" (Appleby, 2005, p. 896; Boyer, 2005, p. 984; Cayton et al., 2003, p. 1024). In reality, armed conflict is the product of human agency where policymakers use violence as an instrument to meet political, economic, and ideological imperatives, taking tremendous risks with human lives.

Although textbooks make fleeting references to foreign policy doctrines, they do not explore the assumptions on which those doctrines are based or their relation to other foreign policies. For instance, textbooks do not present the Vietnam War in the context of an evolving U.S. foreign policy that has changed from the nineteenth-century doctrines of manifest destiny and expansionism to twentieth-century doctrines of progressive imperialism, containment, and most recently, the twenty-first century policy of preventive war. Although each foreign policy has had different assumptions and goals, each permutation has projected U.S. power into increasingly distant lands (McDougall, 1997). During the Cold War alone, containment policy, which was designed to halt communist expansion through fighting a series of limited wars, led the United States to dispatch its military to intervene, disrupt, or quell socialist movements in Greece (1947), Vietnam (1953–1975), Guatemala (1954), Laos (1957–1963), Congo (1960–1964), Cuba (1961), Dominican Republic (1963), Cambodia (1970), Chile (1973), Angola (1976), El Salvador (1980), and Panama (1989). Vietnam represents the longest, deadliest, and most expensive of the United States' Cold War military adventures.

A critical examination of policy statements and memorandums underscores how the Vietnam War was a product of human agency, where the Eisenhower, Kennedy, Johnson, and Nixon administrations, working with limited information and no international support, gradually escalated the Vietnam War.

Rather than rely on textbook accounts, teachers and students can explore the historical record to gain a full appreciation about the ideas, motivations, and mindsets that create war. Electronic databases of historical documents on the Vietnam War allow teachers unprecedented opportunities to examine the historical record and the decisions that led to escalation and eventually withdrawal. *The Foreign Relations of the United States (FRUS)* is the official historical record of major policy statements and actions from the Department of Defense, Central

Intelligence Agency, and National Security Council. Documentary evidence about policy decisions made by the Eisenhower, Kennedy, Johnson, and Nixon-Ford administrations can be found online (www. state.gov/r/pa/ho/frus). Drawing upon these documents, teachers and students can chronicle the evolution of American foreign policy as it relates to the Vietnam War, from the end of World War II to the fall of Saigon in 1975. *The Pentagon Papers* also provides a glimpse into the U.S. raids on North Vietnam, the Kennedy administration's role in installing and later assassinating Ngo Dinh Diem, the illegal U.S. bombings of the neutral countries of Laos and Cambodia, as well as Kennedy's and Johnson's efforts to withhold critical information from the American public. By attending to the documents, teachers render war as a human endeavor, a product of a complex set of political decisions and military actions with consequences for the United States and the people of Southeast Asia.

International Law Provides a Basis to Study Acts of War

If students are to become active citizens capable of breaking through the hegemonic rhetoric offered by textbooks, acts of war must be situated within the larger context of international institutions. Moral attitudes toward war have changed throughout time, and continue to do so. Henri Dunant, founder of the Red Cross, created the First Geneva Convention in 1864. This convention was created to offer protection to the sick and wounded in a time of war. Since 1864, the Red Cross has added conventions addressing treatment of the wounded, prisoners of war, and protection of cultural property (Geneva Conventions, 2006). The Geneva Conventions can be used in the classroom to outline the rules of war established by the International Red Cross. For instance, Conventions III and IV, adopted in 1949, address prisoners of war and the protection of civilians. They state:

> III. Prisoners of war must be treated humanely. Specifically, prisoners must not be subject to torture or medical or scientific experiments of any kind. They must also be protected against violence, intimidation, insults, and public curiosity. The display of POWs is also prohibited.
>
> IV. Civilians are not to be subject to attack. This includes direct attacks on civilians and indiscriminate attacks against areas in which civilians are present.
>
> There is to be no destruction of property unless justified by military necessity. Civilians must not be raped, tortured, or enslaved. (Geneva Conventions, 2006, online)

Rather than rely on textbook narratives, teachers can use these international standards to investigate whether U.S. actions in the Vietnam and the present wars in Iraq and Afghanistan comply with international law. With respect to the Vietnam War, students can investigate the massacres at Hue and My Lai; as well as the U.S. Phoenix Program, which has been described as a program designed to "kill, capture, or make to defect" Vietnamese civilians suspected of assisting the North Vietnamese and Viet Cong (Valentine, 1990, p. 13). When studying Iraq, students can use the Geneva Conventions to determine whether or not the civilian killings at Haditha, or alleged abuses at American military prisons at Abu Graib and Guantanamo Bay violated the third and fourth Geneva Conventions. Government reports, public testimony, firsthand accounts, and photographs can be used as primary sources. Teachers who draw upon international law for historical inquiry provide students with a baseline to judge the military policies and actions. This baseline empowers students to examine the past through an alternative framework that is not tainted by patriotic rhetoric and not dominated by the voice of elected officials or the corporate media's interpretations.

The Media Plays an Important Role in Building Consensus for War

Much like the textbook market, the last 2 decades has marked an intense period of consolidation in the U.S. media where conglomerates like News Corporation, Time Warner, and Disney have significantly increased their holdings in television, film, newspapers, magazines, book publishing, and Internet sites. The Telecommunications Act of 1996 lifted the cap on the number of radio stations a private company could hold (it had previously been 40). Clear Channel Inc. owns more than 1,500 radio stations nationwide. These trends raise questions about the relationship between these media conglomerates and the degree to which they are willing to risk revenues by offering critical reports that corporate advertisers may find offensive.

A cursory review of the corporate media's coverage of the war in Iraq begs questions about the quality of news coverage. In 2002 and 2003, the American media relied almost exclusively on the Bush Administration for information about the emerging crisis in the Middle East. In his analysis of 414 stories on Iraq that aired on ABC, CBS, and NBC from September 4, 2002 to February 7, 2003, Andrew Tyndall found that the majority originated from the White House, Pentagon, and State Department, while only 34 stories originated from other sources (Schecther, 2003, p. 95). The print media also served the Bush Administration by taking up the banner for war while silencing antiwar voices in the newspapers. Russell Mokhiber and Robert Weissman found that in the months prior to the war, the *Washington Post*'s editorial page became "an outpost for the Defense Department":

> Over the six-month period from September through February, the leading newspaper in the nation's capital . . . editorialized twenty-six times in favor of war. It has sometimes been critical of the Bush Administration, it has sometimes commented on developments in the drive to war without offering an opinion on the case for war itself, but it has never offered a peep against military action in Iraq. (Schechter, 2003, p. 96)

Rather than provide a balanced view of the impending conflict, the media's coverage may have contributed to the creation of a confused citizenry. In 2003, the Program of International Policy Attitudes (PIPA) released a study demonstrating that in the months after the United States invaded Iraq, 24% of Americans believed weapons of mass destruction had been found in Iraq, 25% believed that world opinion supported the U.S. invasion, and 49% of those polled believed that the "US . . . found clear evidence that Saddam Hussein was working closely with the Al-Qaeda terrorist organization" (Program of International Policy Attitudes [PIPA], 2003, p. 3). These misperceptions were dependent on the source of the news. Whereas only 23% of people who relied on NPR and PBS for the news held one or more of these three misperceptions, 80% of those who relied on FOX news believed in one of these three key misperceptions. The PIPA study also revealed that among Bush supporters, those who followed the news "very closely" were 14% more likely to believe in one of these three misperceptions and 33% more likely to support the war than those who did not follow the news "closely at all" (PIPA, 2003, p. 20).

If passively consuming media broadcasts manufactures consent and produces a misinformed, confused citizenry, then we must teach our children how to become literate in critically evaluating print and electronic media. Elizabeth Thoman, founder of the Center for Media Literacy (CML), suggests that teachers must instruct students in the basic concepts of media literacy. She relates that at the core of media literacy is

> basic higher-order critical thinking skills—for example, knowing how to identify key concepts, how to make connections between multiple ideas, how to ask pertinent questions, formulate a response, identify fallacies—that form the very foundation of intellectual freedom and full citizenship in a democratic society. (Thoman & Jolls, 2005, p. 6)

CML's inquiry-based 7–12 curriculum is predicated on five core concepts:

1. All media messages are "constructed."
2. Media messages are constructed using a creative language with its own rules.
3. Different people experience the same media message differently.
4. Media have embedded values and points of view.
5. Most media messages are organized to gain profit and/or power. (Thoman & Jolls, 2005, pp. 23–27)

These concepts address who produces media messages, the creative techniques used to get the public's attention, how messages might be interpreted by different groups of people, the values, lifestyles, and points of views represented or omitted from a message, and the purpose for sending the message. These concepts can be used to develop engaging classroom instructional activities that empower students to deconstruct the ways in which the media depicts war. Taken together, applying these concepts will assist students in developing the skills necessary to critically analyze how the media constructs news stories and builds consensus for war.

Voices of Opposition Offer Opportunities to Learn About War

American history is replete with examples of historical figures who, through the application of logic and reason, challenged preemptive military action. By attending to these dissenting voices, we expand the artificial boundaries placed on studying war and treat loyal dissent as a legitimate subject of inquiry, and for some, an act of patriotism. For example, on December 22, 1847, Abraham Lincoln delivered his first speech to the House of Representatives challenging President Polk to defend his rationale for waging war against Mexico. In this speech, Lincoln demanded that Polk explain

> Whether the spot of soil on which the blood of our citizens was shed . . . was or was not within the territories of Spain . . . from the treaty of 1819 [and] Whether the *People* of that settlement, did or did not, flee from the approach of the United States Army, leaving unprotected their homes and their growing crops, *before* the blood was shed. (Lincoln, 1847, p. 159)

This was the same war during which Henry David Thoreau, perhaps America's most influential philosopher, was imprisoned for refusing to pay his poll taxes to support what he thought was an unjust war. Four decades later Mark Twayne wrote *War Prayer*, an essay highlighting the blatant hypocrisy between American Judeo–Christian principles and the death, destruction, and suffering inflicted upon the Cuban people in the Spanish-American war.

More recently, establishment figures such as Senators Gruening, Morse, and Fulbright; and George Ball and Daniel Ellsworth, as well as antiestablishment figures such as Martin Luther King Jr., Muhammad Ali, Noam Chomsky, Howard Zinn, Susan Sontag, and John Kerry provide teachers and students with opportunities to learn about the multiple positions for opposing the Vietnam War. In the run-up to the U.S. invasion of Iraq, President Jimmy Carter (2003) argued that a war with Iraq would not be a just war because diplomatic options were available before the invasion, American weapons fail to discriminate between combatants and noncombatants, and the Bush Administration failed to gain legitimate authority from the United Nations Security Council before attacking.

When we include voices of opposition, we demonstrate to students that each citizen has a right (and responsibility) to actively investigate and question the motives and justifications for armed conflict. Acknowledging voices of dissent also gives students permission to go beyond the traditional pedagogy that cites causes *for* war, effectively justifying war-making. Furthermore, and perhaps most importantly, voices of opposition provide students opportunities to freely examine the reasons for *and* against military action, complicating the historical record, forcing students to engage in historical thinking, and opening doors to deliberation and democratic discourse.

The Government Uses Political Language to Stifle Debate

In 1946, George Orwell wrote, "Political language . . . is designed to make lies sound truthful and murder respectable, and give the appearance of solidarity to pure wind" (Orwell, 1946, p. 8). Orwell was particularly concerned with the powerful ways in which abstract words like *democracy*, *freedom*, *patriotic*, and *justice* can be used to anesthetize the mind and build political conformity for almost any action, regardless of merit or moral value. He explains that words are regularly used as political instruments that deceive the populace and conceal political motivations and controversial actions. This corruption of the English language can be observed in the Bush and Obama administrations' political rhetoric that intentionally employs vague words like *terrorist*, *tyrant*, *weapons of mass destruction*, *insurgents*, *democracy*, as well as countless other terms mindlessly repeated in official government statements and disseminated in newspapers and television broadcasts. Never mind international law, civilian casualties, or the fact that Iraq's estimated petroleum reserves are second only to those of Saudi Arabia; we are told that the war in Iraq is fought to protect us against terrorist threats and promote democracy abroad (Klare, 2002, pp. 39, 45). Such words serve to simplify political conflict, obscure violations of international laws, and mask military aggression and civilian casualties.

In an effort to grasp how the government uses the media to convey official information, teachers and students can deconstruct such messages by looking for creative language, symbols, and images that are repeated in government statements. For example, teachers can lead students in analyzing the language used in the Gulf of Tonkin Resolution (1964) and the Resolution on Iraq (2002). The defensive language of the Tonkin Resolution (which is quoted in all of the American history textbooks) grants President Johnson the authority "to take all necessary measures to repel any armed attack against the forces of the United States and to prevent further aggression" (Hallin, 1986, p. 19). It is almost identical to the political language used in the Iraq Resolution authorizing President Bush "to use the Armed Forces of the United States as he determines to be necessary and appropriate in order to defend the national security of the United States against the continuing threat posed by Iraq; and enforce all relevant United Nations Security Council Resolutions regarding Iraq" (The White House, 2006, online). These simple analyses can better prepare students to identify how language is used as a political instrument to build consensus, and to instill the skills that will aid them in searching for the motivations behind the message.

Corporate Textbooks Promote the Myth of War

Perhaps the most powerful way to puncture the myth of war is to problematize textbook narratives. Podeh (2002) used eight criteria to investigate the structure, tone, and perspectives of Israeli high school textbook depiction of the Arab-Israeli conflict. As a world history teacher, I use a modified version of Podeh's categorical analysis to study textbook depictions of the Crusades, the Columbian Exchange, the Mexican-American War, Spanish-American War, Vietnam War, and the U.S. invasion of Iraq. My modified categories of analysis are:

- *Chronological Accuracy*: What dates, time periods, and other historical events are offered in the textbook's presentation of the war? When does the textbook suggest that the conflict was officially initiated and when did it officially end? What other related historical events and/or circumstances are offered or not offered within the textbook's presentation?
- *Events Centrality and Marginalization*: What events are offered as central to the conflict and what events are marginalized? Are some events presented, in pictures or print, in a distorted way? Have any related events been omitted?
- *Voices—Whose Perspectives Are/Not Represented?* What groups of people (e.g., civilians, politicians, military personnel) are featured in the textbooks' presentation of the war? Which groups are quoted or featured in pictures? Do the text, quotations, and pictures seem sympathetic to one group? Do the text, quotations, and pictures serve to dehumanize one or both groups?
- *Tone*: Taken as a whole, do the categories of analysis, tone of the narrative, nature of the images, and placement within the book serve to offer an unbiased, informative depiction of the Vietnam War?
- *Lessons*: What lessons can be drawn from the textbook's depiction of this war? Who is to blame? How was the end of the conflict brought about? What were the long-term consequences of the conflict?

Unlike standards-based learning, which emphasizes passive acceptance of hegemonic textbook narratives, Podeh's analysis makes the textbook the object of analysis. By attending to textbook narratives' structure, context, and perspective, it treats history as a problematic human construction, shaped by the authors' subjective position as well as publishers' best efforts to create noncontroversial textbooks. Resituating textbooks, it illuminates the multiple ways in which the history of military conflict can be told and rightly acknowledges the function that textbooks play in socializing students into taking positions, dehumanizing our foes, and assigning blame for war.

What I have outlined is an emancipatory pedagogy that prepares students with the skills and disposition to identify injustice and work toward improving the common good. Although it is significantly different from the present system of standards-based education, emphasizing rote instruction evaluated by paper-and-pencil exams, it is not a new or radical doctrine. In fact, it is a return to the basic tenets of history education that were laid out in the National History Standards of 1996. These standards explicitly stated that historical study should reach beyond the study of facts presented in textbooks, and allow students to actively examine the historical record for themselves. Again, the point is to teach children to develop competencies in asking questions, conducting research, analyzing information, and building knowledge about their world, and their place in it:

> Properly taught, history develops capacities for analysis and judgment. It reveals the ambiguity of choice, and promotes wariness about quick, facile solutions which have so often brought human suffering in their wake. History fosters understanding of paradox and a readiness to distinguish between that which is beyond and that which is within human control, between the inevitable and the contingent. It trains students to detect bias, to weigh evidence, and to evaluate judgments, to sniff out spurious appeals to history by partisan pleaders, and distinguish between anecdote and analysis. (NCHS, 1996, p. 7)

What I am suggesting is a more robust democratic form of history education designed to support an active, informed citizenry that not only understands the past, but also sees itself as having a historical presence "that can reflect upon itself, that knows itself as a presence, but that can also take stock of, compare, evaluate, give value to, decide, break with, and dream" (Freire, 1998, p. 26).

As educators we must reclaim our classrooms as public spaces, and work to create opportunities for students to engage the past, develop critical sensibilities, and challenge the assumptions on which the myth of war is based. When we choose to break from the tyranny of standards-based learning, classrooms are elevated from sites of indoctrination to forums of public deliberation, where teachers and students ask questions, search for answers, develop new interpretations, and defend their conclusions with logic and reason. This understanding of history education shapes the lessons I offer on the Vietnam War, located at end of this book (see the Appendix). Each lesson starts with a provocative question followed by historical documents, and guided questions designed to initiate classroom deliberation. These lessons throw open the doors to free inquiry, embrace historical complexity, and demand rigorous intellectual work.

CONCLUSION

Speaking to the American Society of Newspaper Editors in 1953, President Dwight Eisenhower predicted the perils of unchecked military spending and the stockpiling of weapons. In his now famous speech titled, "The Chance for Peace," Eisenhower boldly explained how a devotion to arms drained a nation's wealth, sapping it strength and creativity, ultimately leading to "a life of perpetual fear and tension." Comparing the costs of military armaments to peacetime expenditures, he rationalized that

> Every gun that is made, every warship launched, every rocket fired signifies, in the final sense, a theft from those who hunger and are not fed, those who are cold and are not clothed. This world in arms is not spending money alone. It is spending the sweat of its laborers, the genius of its scientists, the hopes of its children. The cost of one modern heavy bomber is this: a modern brick school in more than 30 cities. It is two fine, fully equipped hospitals. . . . We pay for a single destroyer with new homes that could have housed more than 8,000 people. This is, I repeat, the best way of life to be found on the road the world has been taking. This is not a way of life at all, in any true sense. Under the cloud of threatening war, it is humanity hanging from a cross of iron. (Eisenhower, 1953, paras. 27 & 28)

President Eisenhower's fear of a "world armed against itself" is something to be taken seriously (para 80).

With the exception of infectious disease, modern industrial warfare has been the deadliest force of the 20th century. Niall Ferguson explains that "between 167 million and 188 million people died because of organized violence in the 20th century—as many as one in every 22 deaths in that period" (Ferguson, 2006, p. 61).

The outlook for the next century is not encouraging. There are presently 650 million small arms and light weapons in the world with another 8 million produced annually (MacDonald, 2006). At the time of this writing, an estimated 42 military conflicts are being fought around the world, 8 considered major military conflicts where more than 1,000 people are killed each year (Global Security.org, "*The World at War*," 2008). By 2020, it has been predicted that more people will be killed from armed conflict than infectious disease (Murray & Lopez, 1997).

As the battles to exert American control over Iraq and Afghanistan become increasingly costly in both blood and treasure, educators are faced with a civic dilemma: We can choose to be instruments of the state and continue to rely on textbook narratives that distort history, ignore controversy, and promote the myth of war; or we can choose to exercise human agency and teach our students to think critically about the justification for and execution of American wars. Teaching critically about American foreign policy and questioning the myth of war requires moral and civic courage. By transcending political rhetoric and focusing on evidence and testimony, and attending to those who are in a position to know, it strips away the hegemonic veneer and reveals war for what it is. This form of inquiry will, without doubt, be misconstrued by some as antipatriotic, particularly at a time when the production of arms is one of the soluble sectors of the faltering American economy, military spending has reached unprecedented levels, and the Pentagon has come to rely on American schools to provide the next generation of warriors. Nevertheless, democratic citizenship requires social studies educators to embrace this task, and prepare students to intelligently engage these critical issues.

For certain, a critical examination of textbooks, the historical record, and media stories will offer myriad opportunities for students to learn about modern war. Doing history in this manner illuminates the tentative nature of knowing and leaves students with more questions than answers. Teachers will find this approach difficult, if not impossible, as it sets aside the standardized curricula, dispenses with history textbooks' official interpretations, and opens new routes for free inquiry. Each student will apply a new set of experiences and a unique way of knowing to the study of history. The learning outcomes will be unpredictable, and there will be no patent responses or official interpretations. Authentic forms of assessment will require students to learn how to freely ask questions, interact with the historical record, defend their positions with logic and reason, and work to construct their own understandings of the world. These types of classroom activities lead to a richer, stronger form of patriotism where teachers arm students with the skills and knowledge to effectively engage their fellow citizens and elected leaders in an open, informed debate about American foreign policy and the legitimacy of American wars.

APPENDIX

Lessons on the Vietnam War

CLASSROOM LESSON 1:
EXPLORING THE U.S. COLD WAR MIND-SET

Central Question: What were the major assumptions behind the U.S. Cold War mind-set?

Objectives:

1. Students will explore how U.S. officials viewed the Soviet Union's goals in the post–World War II era.
2. Students will analyze U.S. policy to meet this perceived threat of Soviet world domination.
3. Students will determine how individual actors can influence foreign policy.

Historical Documents:

Kennan, G. (1947, July). "The Sources of Soviet Conduct." *Foreign Affairs.* (Available online at www.foreignaffairs.org/19470701 faessay25403/x/the-sources-of-soviet-conduct.html)
National Security Council 68: United States Objectives and Programs for National Security. (January 31, 1951). (Available online at www.fas.org/irp/offdocs/nsc-hst/nsc-68-4.htm)

Introduction:

1. Provide students with George Kennan's "The Sources of Soviet Conduct."
2. Have students make a list of the adjectives Kennan uses to describe the Soviet Union.
3. Taken together, what kind of picture does Kennan paint of the Soviet Union?
4. What evidence does Kennan use in describing the Soviet Union's policy of expansion?

Guided Practice:

1. Provide students with a hard copy of NSC-68.
2. Have students make a T-chart, detailing how NSC-68 defines the "fundamental purpose of the United States" and "the fundamental design of the Kremlin."
3. Ask students to identify the three "courses of action" outlined in NSC-68. How do these courses of action differ?
4. Request each student to evaluate the pros and cons of each action.

Classroom Debate/Discussion:

1. What are the major assumptions behind Kennan's statements on the Soviet Union?
2. To what degree do Kennan's thoughts on the Soviet Union influence NSC-68?
3. What are the implications behind each of the United States' courses of action?
4. Are there other possible courses of action?
5. What if Kennan's assumptions, as well as those found within NSC-68, are wrong?

CLASSROOM LESSON 2:
THE GULF OF TONKIN CRISIS

Central Question: What role, if any, did the U.S. covert war against North Vietnam play in the Gulf of Tonkin crisis?

Objectives:

1. Students will learn about the U.S. covert war against North Vietnam that preceded the Gulf of Tonkin Resolution.
2. Students will compare the textbook narrative and President Johnson's Gulf of Tonkin Resolution with the historical records describing covert U.S. operations.
3. Student will assess textbook treatments of the Gulf of Tonkin crisis.

Documents:

The Gulf of Tonkin Resolution. (A high-resolution copy is available at www.ourdocuments.gov/doc.php?doc=98)

The Pentagon Papers. Evolution of the War: Military Pressures against North Vietnam Action and Debate, February-June 1964. (A copy of the original papers on the Gulf of Tonkin is available at www.vietnam.ttu.edu/star/images/213/2130316005.pdf)

Introduction:

1. Have students use their textbooks to make a time line of the Vietnam War leading up to the Gulf of Tonkin Crisis.
2. Ask students to identify the quotes used to describe the crisis.
3. Ask students, "Whose perspective is represented in their textbook?"

Guided Practice:

1. Have students read Section I, subsections A and B of "Evolution of the War: Military Pressures Against North Vietnam Action and Debate."
2. As they read these subsections, have them list the types of covert operations the U.S. military carried out prior to the Gulf of Tonkin crisis in August 1964.
3. Have students write these operations on the time line generated from the textbook.
4. Have students read the Gulf of Tonkin Resolution.

Classroom Debate/Discussion:

1. Ask students how these events support or contradict their textbooks' description of the Gulf of Tonkin crisis. How has their understanding changed?
2. What role do U.S. covert operations play in the Gulf of Tonkin crisis? Do they matter?
3. What are the contradictions between the historical record and Johnson's Gulf of Tonkin Resolution?
4. What information is missing from textbook accounts? What is missing from the Gulf of Tonkin Resolution? What do these omissions mean for the American public?

CLASSROOM LESSON 3:
THE MEDIA AND WAR

Central Question: What is the relationship between the media and the military in times of war?

Objectives:

1. Students will learn about how the American media initially reported the Gulf of Tonkin crisis and the U.S. invasion of Iraq.
2. Students will learn how to actively analyze media stories.

Documents:

Textbook
Front page of the August 4, 1964 *New York Times.*
Front page of the March 21, 2003 *New York Times.*
Thoman, E., & Jolls, T. (2005). *Literacy for the 21st century.*
    Malibu, CA: Center for Media Literacy. (Available online at
    www.medialit.org/pdf/mlk/01_MLKorientation.pdf)

Introduction:

1. Ask students to generate a list of people that would be impacted
   by war (e.g., civilians, international leaders, American soldiers,
   enemy soldiers, etc.).
2. Have students read the Center for Media Literacy's five Core
   Concepts. (Available online at www.medialit.org/pdf/mlk/14A_
   CCKQposter.pdf)
3. What do these concepts suggest about the media?

Guided Practice:

1. Have students read the front page of the August 4, 1964 *New York
   Times.*
2. As they read the article, have students consider the following
   questions:

   • Who created the message?
   • What creative techniques are used to attract my attention?
   • How might different people understand the message
     differently?
   • What values, lifestyles, and points of view are presented in,
     or omitted from this message?

3. Repeat the same procedure for the front page of the March 21,
   2003 *New York Times.*

Classroom Debate/Discussion:

1. How were these two messages, separated by nearly 4 decades,
   constructed? Were there significant similarities and/or differences
   in the way that the stories were constructed?
2. Ask students how alternative pictures, quotations, and sources
   of information might convey a different message. Was there
   anything missing?
3. Given the message's construction, what function does the message
   serve (e.g., building consent for war, informing the public of recent
   developments, initiating a public debate, instilling fear, etc.).

4. What are the implications for this type of reporting in a democratic society?

CLASSROOM LESSON 4:
ATTENDING TO VOICES OF OPPOSITION

Central Question: How do voices/acts of opposition improve our understanding of war?

Objectives:

1. Students will understand that war-making is often met by resistance.
2. Student will explore the nature of symbolic acts of resistance.
3. Students will learn about the reasons for opposing the Vietnam War.

Documents:

King Jr., M.L. (1967). *Beyond Vietnam*. (Available online at www.stan-ford.edu/group/King/publications/speeches/Beyond_Vietnam.pdf)

Kerry, J. (1971). *Testimony before the Senate Foreign Relations Committee*. (Available online at http://facultystaff.richmond.edu/~ebolt/history398/JohnKerryTestimony.html)

Photos:

Malcolm Brown's award-winning photograph of Thich Quang Duc's self-immolation.

Introduction:

1. Explain to students that protest is a symbolic act that seeks to build opposition to war.
2. Show students Malcolm Brown's award-winning photograph of Thich Quang Duc's self-immolation.
3. Record initial reactions and observations.
4. Ask students to consider three components of the picture: (1) the context, (2) the intended message, and (3) the impact on the international audience.

Guided Practice:

1. Explain to students that war is often met by resistance, for a variety of reasons.
2. Divide students into two groups. Have the first group read Martin Luther King Jr.'s *Beyond Vietnam* and the second group read John Kerry's *Testimony Before the Senate Foreign Relations Committee*.

3. Have each group make a list of reasons King and Kerry provide for opposing the Vietnam War.
4. For each speech, ask students to consider the context, the intended message, and the impact.

Classroom Debate/Discussion:

1. Ask the class if they find King and/or Kerry's statements compelling.
2. Would King's and/or Kerry's calls for opposition resonate with some groups more than others? Why or why not?
3. What are the implications/dangers for opposing war?
4. Ask students to consider Zinn's quote "Dissent is the highest form of patriotism."

CLASSROOM LESSON 5:
APPLYING INTERNATIONAL LAW TO WAR

Central Question: What is the necessity of having laws that regulate warfare?

Objectives:

1. Students will be introduced to the First, Second, Third, and Fourth Geneva Conventions, the basis of international law regulating war.
2. Students will read Ron Ridenhour's letter to Congress, detailing reports of the My Lai Massacre.
3. Students will explore and evaluate the My Lai and My Khe massacres vis-à-vis the Fourth Geneva Convention.

Documents:

International Humanitarian Law: The Essential Rules. This is a summary of the Four Geneva Conventions offered by the International Committee of the Red Cross. (Available online at www.icrc.org/Web/Eng/siteeng0.nsf/html/5ZMEEM)

Ridenhour, R. (March 29, 1969). Congressional letter detailing reports of My Lai massacre. (Available online at www.law.umkc. edu/faculty/projects/FTRIALS/mylai/ridenhour_ltr.html)

Video:

Morris, E. (Producer). (2004). *The Fog of War* [Film]. United States: Sony Pictures.

Introduction:

1. Show students Scene 13 (Lesson 5) of *Fog of War* (2004).
2. What does Robert McNamara mean when he says, "Proportionality should be a guideline in war?"
3. What evidence can you provide to either support or refute McNamara's statement, "The human race has not grappled with the rules of war."
4. Respond to McNamara's question, "Do morals depend on who wins war?"

Guided Practice:

1. Have students read the *International Humanitarian Law: The Essential Rules*.
2. What protections do these conventions provide civilians? Are they necessary?
3. Distribute Ron Ridenhour's congressional letter detailing reports of the My Lai massacre.
4. Does Ridenhour's statement suggest that the rules of war were honored at My Lai? If not, how were they broken?

Classroom Debate/Discussion:

1. Is it possible to protect civilian life? What makes it difficult to do so?
2. Was Ridenhour doing the right thing publicizing what he learned about My Lai?
3. If you were a member of Congress, how would you respond to Ridenhour's letter?

CLASSROOM LESSON 6:
EXAMINING NIXON'S "PEACE WITH HONOR"

Central Questions: (1) What were the circumstances that led to American withdrawal? (2) How did the Paris Peace agreements meet the needs of the warring factions?

Objectives:

1. Students will explore Nixon's reasons for continuing the Vietnam War in 1969.
2. Students will examine the military and political developments that led Nixon to move toward a negotiated peace in 1971.

3. Students will understand the terms of the Paris Peace Agreement (January 27, 1973).

Documents:

Richard Nixon speech delivered November 3, 1969. (Audio file or print copy available online at www.presidency.ucsb.edu/ws/index. php?pid=2303#)

Richard Nixon speech delivered April 7, 1971. (Audio file or print copy available online at www.presidency.ucsb.edu/ws/index. php?pid=2972&st=&st1=)

Richard Nixon speech delivered January 23, 1973. (Audio file or print copy available online at www.presidency.ucsb.edu/ws/index. php?pid=3808&st=&st1=)

Paris Peace Accords signed January 27, 1973. (Print copy available online at www.aiipowmia.com/sea/ppa1973.html)

Introduction:

1. Have students view the nationally televised speech Nixon delivered November 3, 1969.
2. As they listen, have students list Nixon's reasons to continue the war.
3. Given these reasons, what would it take for Nixon to end the war?

Guided Practice:

1. Have students view the nationally televised speech Nixon delivered on April 7, 1971.
2. What reasons does Nixon give for withdrawing 265,000 American forces?
3. What progress does Nixon site for his claim that Vietnamization has succeeded?
4. Has he met the goals he articulated in 1969?
5. What reason does Nixon give for refusing to withdraw?

Classroom Debate/Discussion:

1. Divide the students into four groups: U.S. representatives, South Vietnamese nationalists, Viet Cong, and North Vietnamese.
2. Have students read the Paris Peace Accords, signed January 27, 1973.
3. Assuming their assigned roles, what is their reaction to the Paris Peace Agreement?
4. Who wins? Who loses?

High School
History Textbooks

Appleby, J., Brinkley, A., Broussard, A., McPherson, J., & Ritchie, D. (2005). *The American vision*. New York: McGraw-Hill.

Boorstin, D. J., & Kelley, B. M. (2005). *A history of the United States*. Needham, MA: Pearson Prentice Hall.

Boyer, P. (2005). *The American nation*. New York: Holt, Rhinehart, & Winston.

Cayton, A., Perry, E. I., Reed, L., & Winkler, A. (2003). *America: Pathways to the present*. Needham, MA: Prentice-Hall.

Danzer, G., Klor de Alva, J. J., Wilson, L., & Woloch, N. (1998). *The Americans*. Boston: McDougall Littell.

Ellis, E. B., & Esler, A. (2005). *World history: Connections to today*. Needham, MA: Pearson Prentice Hall.

Farah, M., & Karls, A. B. (1999). *World history: The human experience*. New York: Glencoe McGraw-Hill.

Holt, Rinehart, & Winston. (1999). *World history: Continuity and change*. New York: Author.

Holt, Rinehart, & Winston. (2000). *World history: People and nations*. New York: Author.

Holt, Rinehart, & Winston. (2005). *World history: The human journey*. New York: Author.

McDougall Littell. (1999). *World history: Patterns of interaction*. Evanston, IL: Author.

Nash, G. B. (2002). *American odyssey: The United States in the 20th century*. New York: Glencoe McGraw-Hill.

References

Abella, A. (2008). *Soldiers of reason: The Rand corporation and the rise of the American empire*. New York: Harcourt.

Abrams, D. (2008). *Dates of elementary- and intermediate-level state assessments for the 2008–09 school year*. Retrieved January 11, 2009, from www.emsc.nysed.gov/osa/schedules/elerev08-09.pdf

Agostinone-Wilson, F. (2008, March 14). *Education toward war*. Paper presented at the Rouge Forum Conference, Louisville, KY.

Alterman, E. (2004). *When presidents lie: A history of official deception and its consequences*. New York: Penguin.

American Textbook Council. (2006). *Widely adopted textbooks*. Retrieved April 29, 2009, from www.historytextbooks.org/adopted.htm

America's Army. (2009). *The official army game*. Retrieved April 25, 2009, from www.americasarmy.com

Anderson, D. L. (Ed.). (1998). *Facing My Lai: Moving beyond the massacre*. Lawrence: University of Kansas Press.

Ansary, T. (2004, November/December). *The muddle machine: Confessions of a textbook writer*. Retrieved March 30, 2006, from www.edutopia.org/magazine/ed1article.php?id=Art _1195&issue=nov_04

Apple, M. (1979). *Ideology and curriculum*. New York: Routledge & Kegan Paul.

Apple, M. (2000). *Official knowledge: Democratic education in a conservative age*. New York: Routledge.

Appy, C. (1999, February 12). The muffling of public memory in post Vietnam America. *The Chronicle of Higher Education, 45*(23), B4–B6.

Aronson, J. (1970). *The press and the Cold War*. New York: Bobbs-Merrill.

Asbury Park Press. (2006, June 12). *Guard recruiters woo educators*. Retrieved June 19, 2006, from www.app.com/apps/pbcs.dll/article?AID=/20060612/NEWS03/606120356/1007/BUSNESS7

Associated Press. (2008, July 15). *Probe of Tillman misinformation goes nowhere*. Retrieved July 15, 2008, from www.latimes.com/news/nationworld/nation/la-na-tillman15-2008jul15,0,246216.story

Association of American Publishers [AAP]. (2006). *Association of American Publishers 2005 statistics*. Retrieved April 20, 2007, from www.publishers.org/industry/2005_annual_report_preface.pdf

Association of American Publishers [AAP]. (2007). *Interactive textbook adoption/open territory map*. Retrieved April 20, 2007, from www.publishers.org/SchoolDiv/textBooks/textBk_01_Map.htm

Association of American Publishers [AAP]. (2009, March). *Association of American publishers 2008 S1 report: Estimated book publishing industry net sales, 2002–2008*. Washington, DC: Author.

Bacevich, A. (2005). *The new American militarism*. New York: Oxford University Press.

Baker, K. (2006). *Stabbed in the back! The past and future of a right-wing myth*. Retrieved January 4, 2009, from www.harpers.org/archive/2006/06/0081080

Barrett, D. M. (Ed.). (1997). *Lyndon B. Johnson Vietnam papers: A documentary collection*. College Station: Texas A&M Press.

Bennett, W. J. (1998). The place to harvest patriots. *The School Administrator, 55*(5), 38–40.

Bennett deMarrais, K., & LeCompte, M. (1995). *The way schools work: A sociological analysis of education*. New York: Longman.

Bilton, M., & Sim, K. (1992). *Four hours in My Lai*. New York: Viking.

Bodnar, J. (1992). *Remaking America: Public memory, commemoration, and patriotism in the twentieth century*. Princeton, NJ: Princeton University Press.

Boggs, C. (2005). *Imperial delusions*. New York: Rowman & Littlefield.

Bragdon, H. W. (1969). Dilemmas of a textbook writer. *Social Education, 33*(3), 292–298.

Brinkley, D. (2004). *Tour of duty: John Kerry and the Vietnam War*. New York: William Morrow.

Caputo, P. (1977). *A rumor of war*. New York: Owl Books.

Carter, J. (2003, March 9). Just war—or a just war? *The New York Times*, pp. 4, 13.

Center for Public Integrity. (2008, January 23). *The war card: Orchestrated deception on the path to war*. Retrieved May 1, 2009, from projects.publicintegrity.org/WarCard

Cheney, L. (1994, October 20). The end of history. *The Wall Street Journal*, p. A22.

Chomsky, N. (1989). *Necessary illusions: Thought control in democratic societies*. Concord, Ontario, Canada: Anansi Press.

Cirincione, J., Mathews, J. T., Orton, A., & Perkovich, G. (2004). *WMDs in Iraq: Evidence and implications*. Washington, DC: Carnegie Endowment for International Peace.

Cohen, J. (2001, May 6). The myth of the media's role in Vietnam. *Fairness and Accuracy in Reporting*. Retrieved on April 24, 2007, from http://www.fair.org/index.php?page=2526

Cohen, R. (1996). Moving beyond the name games: The conservative attack on the U.S. history standards. *Social Education, 60*(1), 49–54.

Cooper, C. (1970). *The lost crusade: America in Vietnam*. New York: Dodd, Mead.

Correll, J. T. (1994, December). Airplanes in the mist. *Air Force Magazine, 77*(12), 2.

Cronkite, W. (1996). *A reporter's life*. New York: Knopf.

Daalder, I., & Lindsay, J. (2003). *America unbound: The Bush revolution in foreign policy*. Washington, DC: The Brookings Institution.

Delfattore, J. (1992). *What Johnny shouldn't read: Textbook censorship in America*. New Haven, CT: Yale University Press.

Dewey, J. (1966). *Democracy and education*. New York: The Free Press.

Draper, T. (1967). *Abuse of power*. New York: Viking Press.

Drea, E. J. (2004). *Tonkin Gulf reappraisal: 40 years later*. Retrieved October 28, 2006, from www.historynet.com/historical_conflicts/3027151

Duiker, W. (1994). *U.S. containment policy and the conflict in Indochina*. Palo Alto, CA: Stanford University Press.

Edison Schools Inc. (2009). *About Edison Schools*. Retrieved January 16, 2009, from www.edisonschools.com/edison-schools/about-us

Education Sector. (2006). *An industry in need of testing*. Retrieved July 3, 2009, from www.educationsector.org/enewsletter/enewsletter_list_more.htm?issue_id=2326

Eisenhower, D. (1953). *The chance for peace*. Dwight D. Eisenhower Memorial Commission. Retrieved September 9, 2009, from http://www.eisenhower-memorial.org/speeches/19530416%20Chance%20for%20Peace.htm

Ellsberg, D. (2002). *Secrets: A memoir of Vietnam and the Pentagon Papers*. New York: Viking.

Engelhardt, T. (1996, January). Fifty years under a cloud. *Harper's Magazine, 292*(1748), 71–77.

Ferguson, N. (2006). The next war of the world. *Foreign Affairs, 85*(5), 61–74.

Fernandes, D. (2007, February 5). *This alien life: Privatized prisons for immigrants*. Retrieved on January 26, 2009, from www.corpwatch.org/article.php?id=14333

Fitzgerald, F. (1972). *Fire in the lake: The Vietnamese and Americans in the Vietnam War*. New York: Little, Brown.

Fitzgerald, F. (1979). *America revised: History schoolbooks in the twentieth century*. Boston: Little, Brown.

Freire, P. (1993). *Pedagogy of the oppressed*. New York: Continuum.

Freire, P. (1998). *Pedagogy of freedom: Ethics, democracy, and civic courage*. New York: Rowman & Littlefield.

Fulbright, J. W. (1966). *The arrogance of power*. New York: Random House.

Fulbright, J. W., & Tillman, S. (1989). *The price of empire*. New York: Pantheon.

Galloway, J. (1970). *Gulf of Tonkin resolution*. Cranbury, NJ: Associated University Press.

Gelb, L. H., & Betts, R. K. (1979). *The Irony of Vietnam: The system worked*. Washington, DC: The Brookings Institution.

Geneva Conventions. (2006). *A brief history of the laws of war*. Retrieved June 29, 2008, from www.genevaconventions.org

Giap, V. N. (1967). Big victory, great task. In R. Stetler (Ed.), *The military art of people's war: Selected writings of General Vo Nguyen* (pp. 285–307). New York: Monthly Review Press.

Gibson, J. W. (1986). *The perfect war: Technowar in Vietnam*. New York: Atlantic Monthly Press.

GlobalIssues.org. (2008). *World military spending*. Retrieved April 27, 2009, from www.globalissues.org/Geopolitics/ArmsTrade/Spending.asp-InContext USMilitarySpendingVersusRestoft

GlobalSecurity.org. (2008). *The world at war*. Retrieved June 22, 2008 from www.globalsecurity.org/military/world/war/index .html

Goldberger, P. (1996, February 11). Historical shows on trial: Who judges? *The New York Times*, pp. 2.1, 2.26.

Gramsci, A. (2005). *Selections from the prison notebooks of Antonio Gramsci* (Q. Hoare & G. N. Smith, Trans.). New York: International Publishers. (Original work published 1971)

Greider, W. (1998). *Fortress America: The American military and the consequences of peace.* New York: Public Affairs.

Gruening, E., & Beaser, H. W. (1968). *Vietnam folly.* Washington, DC: National Press.

Hackworth, D. H., & Sherman, J. (1989). *About face: The odyssey of an American warrior.* New York: Simon & Schuster.

Halberstam, D. (1969). *The best and the brightest.* New York: Ballantine.

Hallin, D. C. (1986). *The uncensored war: The media and Vietnam.* New York: Oxford University Press.

Hammond, W. (1988). *Public affairs: The military and the media, 1962–1968.* Washington, DC: Center for Military History.

Hanson, V. D. (2001). The meaning of Tet. *American Heritage, 52*(3), 44–55.

Hanson, V. D. (2003). Preserving America, man's greatest hope. In *Terrorists, despots, and democracy: What our children need to know* (pp. 23–24). Washington, DC: Thomas B. Fordham Foundation.

Hanyok, R. J. (2005). *Skunks, bogies, silent hounds, and the flying fish: The Gulf of Tonkin mystery, 2–4 August 1964.* Retrieved April 29, 2009, from www.nsa.gov/public_info/_files/gulf_of_tonkin/articles/rel1_skunks_bogies.pdf

Harris, L. (1973). *The anguish of change.* New York: W.W. Norton.

Harwit, M. (1995). Academic freedom in the last act. *The Journal of American History, 82*(3), 1064–1084.

Harwit, M. (1996). *An exhibit denied: Lobbying the history of the Enola Gay.* New York: Springer.

Hedges, C. (2002). *War is a force that gives us meaning.* New York: Anchor Books.

Hedges, C. (2003, April 21). *The press and myths of war.* Retrieved June 21, 2006, from www.thenation.com/doc/20030421/hedges

Herbert, B. (2005, June 16). Uncle Sam really wants you. *The New York Times,* p. A27.

Herr, M. (1978). *Dispatches.* New York: Avon.

Herring, G. (1987). America and Vietnam: The debate continues. *The American Historical Review, 92*(2), 350–362.

Herring, G. (1991). America and Vietnam: The unending war. *Foreign Affairs, 70*(5), 104–120.

Herring, G. (2002a). What kind of war was the Vietnam War? In D. L. Anderson (Ed.), *Facing My Lai: Moving beyond the massacre* (pp. 95–106). Lawrence: University of Kansas Press.

Herring, G. (2002b). *America's longest war: The United States and Vietnam, 1950–1975* (4th ed.). New York: McGraw-Hill.

Hersh, S. M. (1970). *My Lai 4: A report of the massacre and its aftermath.* New York: Random House.

Hersh, S. M. (1972). *Cover-up.* New York: Random House.

Hess, G. (1994). The unending debate: Historians and the Vietnam War. *Diplomatic History, 18*(2), 239–264.

Hess, G. (1997). *Vietnam and the United States: Origins and legacy of war.* New York: Twayne Publishers.

Hirsch, Jr., E. D. (1996). *The schools we need: And why we don't have them.* New York: Doubleday.

Hurdle, J. (2009, February 12). *U.S. judges admit to jailing children for money.* Retrieved on February 12, 2009, from http://uk.reuters.com/article/burning Issues/idUKTRE51B7B320090212?pageNumber=1&virtualBrandChannel=0

Juhnke, J. C., & Hunter, C. M. (2001). *The missing peace: The search for non-violent alternatives in United States history.* Kitchener, Ontario, Toronto: Pandora Press.

Johnson, C. (2004). *The sorrows of empire: Militarism, secrecy, and the end of the republic.* New York: Henry Holt & Company.

Johnson, L. B. (1964). *Radio and television report to the American people following renewed aggression in the Gulf of Tonkin.* Retrieved January 7, 2009, from www.presidency.ucsb.edu/ws/index.php?pid=26418

Johnson, R. D. (1998). *Ernest Gruening and the American dissenting tradition.* Cambridge, MA: Harvard University Press.

Kahin, T. (1979). *Intervention: How America became involved in the Vietnam War.* New York: Knopf.

Kammen, M. (1991). *Mystic chords of memory.* New York: Knopf.

Karnow, S. (1997). *Vietnam: A history.* New York: Penguin.

Katovsky, B., & Carlson, T. (2003). *Embedded: The media at war in Iraq.* Guilford, CT: The Lyons Press.

Kennan, G. (1947). The sources of Soviet conflict. *Foreign Affairs, 25*(4), 566–581.

Kerry, J. F. (1991). Statement before the Senate Foreign Affairs Committee. In W. Capps (Ed.), *The Vietnam reader* (pp. 152–157). New York: Routledge.

Klare, M. (2002). *Resource wars: The new landscape of global conflict.* New York: Henry Holt & Company.

Kohn, R. H. (1995). History and the culture wars: The case of the Smithsonian Institution's Enola Gay exhibition. *The Journal of American History, 82*(3), 1036–1063.

Kolko, G. (1985). *Anatomy of a war: Vietnam, the United States, and the modern historical experience.* New York: Pantheon Books.

Krepinevich, A. F. (1986). *The army and Vietnam.* Baltimore: Johns Hopkins Press.

Lardner, R. (2007, September 19). *180,000 private contractors flood Iraq.* Retrieved December 1, 2008, from www.washingtonpost.com/wpdyn/content/article/2007/09/19/AR2007091901836.html

Laxler, J. (2007). *Empire: A groundwork.* Toronto: Groundwood Books.

Leahey, C. (2004). Examining media coverage: A classroom study of Iraq war news. *Social Education, 68*(4), 280–289.

Leave My Child Alone. (2009). Homepage. Retrieved July 21, 2009, from http://www.leavemychildalone.org/

Lefever, E. (1997, May 21). Vietnam's ghosts. *The Wall Street Journal*, p. A14.

Lembcke, J. (1998). *The spitting image: Myth, memory, and the legacy of Vietnam.* New York: NYU Press.

Lewy, G. (1978). *America in Vietnam*. Oxford: Oxford University Press.

Lincoln, A. (1847). "Spot" resolutions in the U.S. House of Representatives. In D. E. Fehrenbacher (Ed.), *Abraham Lincoln: Speeches and writings, 1832–1858* (pp. 158–159). New York: The Library of America.

Lincoln, A. (1863). *The Gettysburg Address*. Retrieved on January 3, 2009, from www.loc.gov/exhibits/gadd/images/Gettysburg-2.jpg

Lind, M. (1999). *Vietnam: The necessary war*. New York: The Free Press.

Lockheed Martin. (2009). *Lockheed Martin at a glance*. Retrieved April 29, 2009, from www.lockheedmartin.com/aboutus/at_a_glance.html

Loewen, J. (1996). *Lies my teacher told me: Everything your American history textbook got wrong*. New York: Touchstone.

Logevall, F. (1999). *Choosing war: The last chance for peace and the escalation of war in Vietnam*. Los Angeles: The University of California Press.

Lomperis, T. J. (1984). *The war everyone lost—and won: America's intervention in Viet Nam's twin struggles*. Baton Rouge: Louisiana State University Press.

Mabry, L., Poole, J., Redmond, L., & Schultz, A. (2003, July 18). Local impact of state testing in southwest Washington. *Education Policy Analysis Archives, 11*(21). Retrieved January 9, 2009, from http://epaa.asu.edu/epaa/v11n22

MacDonald, R. (2006). Where next for arms control? *Lancet, 368*(9357), 713–714.

Macedo, D. (1994). *Literacies of power*. Boulder, CO: Westview Press.

Marling, K. S., & Wetenhall, J. (1991). *Iwo Jima, monuments, memories, and the American hero*. Cambridge, MA: Harvard University Press.

Mathison, S., & Ross, E. W. (2004). The hegemony of accountability; the corporate-political alliance for control of schools. In E. W. Ross, D. Gabbard, K. Kesson, & S. Mathison (Eds.), *Defending public schools* (Vol. 1, pp. 91–100). Westport, CT: Praeger.

McDougall, W. A. (1997). Back to bedrock: The eight traditions of American statecraft. *Foreign Affairs, 76*(2), 134–146.

McLaren, P. (1998). *Life in schools: An introduction to critical pedagogy in the foundations of education*. New York: Longman.

McMaster, H. R. (1997). *Dereliction of duty: Lyndon Johnson, Robert McNamara, the joint chiefs of staff, and the lies that led to Vietnam*. New York: HarperCollins.

McNamara, R., & VanDeMark, B. (1995). *In Retrospect: The tragedy and lessons of Vietnam*. New York: Random House.

Moise, E. (1996). *Tonkin Gulf and the escalation of the Vietnam War*. Chapel Hill: University of North Carolina Press.

Moon, T., Callahan, C., & Tomlinson, C. (2003, April 28). Effects of state testing programs on elementary schools with high concentrations of student poverty—good news or bad news? *Current Issues in Education, 6*(8). Retrieved January 9, 2009, from http://cie.ed.asu.edu/volume6/number8/

Mosse, G. (1990). *Fallen soldiers: Reshaping the memory of the world wars*. New York: Oxford University Press.

Murray, C. J., & Lopez, A. D. (1997). Alternative projections of mortality and disability by cause, 1990–2020: Global burden of disease study. *The Lancet, 349*(9064), 1498–1504.

Nash, G., Crabtree, C., & Dunn, R. (1997). *History on trial: Culture wars and the teaching of the past.* New York: Knopf.

National Center for History in Schools [NCHS]. (1994). *National standards for United States history.* Los Angeles: University of California at Los Angeles.

National Center for History in Schools [NCHS]. (1996). *National standards for history.* Los Angeles: University of California at Los Angeles.

National Council for the Social Studies. (1994). *Expectations for excellence: Curriculum standards for social studies.* Silver Spring, MD: National Council for Social Studies.

Nelan, B. (1995, April 24). Lessons from the lost war. *Time, 145*(17), 44–45.

New York State Education Department. (1999). *Social studies resource guide with core curriculum.* Albany: Author.

Nobile, P. (Ed.). (1995). *Judgment at the Smithsonian.* New York: Marlowe and Company.

Noddings, N. (2002). *Educating moral people: A caring alternative to character education.* New York: Teachers College Press.

Oberdorfer, D. (1971). *Tet!* New York: Da Capo Press.

O'Brien, S. (1989). How to produce a better Edsel—Writing U.S. history textbooks. *Social Education, 53,* 98–100.

O'Brien, T. (1998). The mystery of My Lai. In D. L. Anderson (Ed.), *Facing My Lai: Moving beyond the massacre* (pp. 171–178). Lawrence: University of Kansas Press.

Orwell, G. (1946). Politics and the English language. In G. Packer (Ed.), *All art is propaganda* (pp. 270–286). Orlando, FL: Harcourt.

Palmer, D. R. (1978). *Summons of the trumpet: U.S.-Vietnam in perspective.* San Rafael, CA: Presidio Press.

The Pentagon Papers: The defense department history of decisionmaking on Vietnam. (1971a). The Senator Gravel edition (Vol. 3). Boston: Beacon.

The Pentagon Papers: The defense department history of decisionmaking on Vietnam. (1971b). The Senator Gravel edition (Vol. 4). Boston: Beacon.

Plato. (1993). *The republic* (R. Waterfield, Trans.). New York: Oxford University Press.

Podeh, E. (2002). *The Arab-Israeli conflict in Israeli history textbooks, 1948–2000.* Westport, CT: Bergin & Garvey.

Podhoretz, N. (1982). *Why we were in Vietnam.* New York: Simon & Schuster.

Porter, D. G. (1974). *The 1968 Hue massacre.* Retrieved on August 4, 2006, from www.chss.montclair.edu/english/furr/porterhue1.html

Program of International Policy Attitudes. (2003). *Misperceptions, the media, and the Iraq war.* Retrieved October 15, 2006, from http://65.109.167.118/pipa/pdf/oct03/IraqMedia_Oct03_rpt.pdf

Prosise, T. O. (1998). The collective memory of the atomic bombings misrecognized as objective history: The case of the public opposition to the national air and space museum's atom bomb exhibit. *Western Journal of Communication, 62*(3), 316–347.

Public Broadcasting System. (2004, April 30). *Sinclair stations pull Nightline Iraq casualties report.* Retrieved July 7, 2008, from www.pbs.org/newshour/updates/abc_04-30-04.html

Public Broadcasting System Nightly Business Report. (2008, February 18). *The new business of education standardized testing.* Retrieved January 15, 2009, from www.pbs.org/nbr/site/onair/transcripts/080218a/

Quality Counts. (2008). *National highlights.* Retrieved July 10, 2008, from http://www.pewcenteronthestates.org/uploadedFiles/NationalHighlights-Report.pdf

Ravitch, D. (2003). *The language police.* New York: Knopf.

Rendall, S., & Broughel, T. (2003). *Amplifying officials, squelching dissent.* Retrieved April 17, 2009, from www.fair.org/index.php?page=1145

Ridenhour, R. (1969). Letter to key public officials describing My Lai massacre. In D. L. Anderson (Ed.), *Facing My Lai: Moving beyond the massacre* (pp. 201–206). Lawrence: University of Kansas Press.

Ridenhour, R. (1993, March). Perpsective on My Lai. *Los Angeles Times*, p. B7.

Riverside Publishing. (2009). *Fall 2008 order form Riverside Scoring Service. The IOWA Tests, forms a, b or c, and Cogat, form 6 scoring packages.* Retrieved January 8, 2009, from www.riverpub.com/products/orderform/IowaCogat-OSS.pdf

Roa, B. (2009). The military invades U.S. schools: How military academies are being used to destroy public education. *AlterNet*, online. Retrieved July 15, 2009, from www.alternet.org/module/printversion/141034

Roper, B. (1977). What public opinion polls said. In P. Braestrup (Ed.), *Big story: How the American press and television reported and interpreted the crisis of Tet 1968 in Washington and Saigon* (Vol. 1, pp. 674–704). Boulder, CO: Westview Press.

Roy, A. (2003, August 24). *The loneliness of Noam Chomsky.* Retrieved May 1, 2009, from www.thehindu.com/thehindu/mag/2003/08/24/stories/2003082400020100.htm

Sacks, P. (2001). *Standardized minds: The high price of American testing culture and what we can do to change it.* New York: Da Capo Press.

Saltman, K. (2004). The securitized student: Meeting the demands of neoliberalism. In E. W. Ross & D. Gabbard (Eds.), *Defending public schools: Education under the security state* (Vol. 1, pp. 157–173). Westport, CT: Praeger.

Sandburg, C. (1916). *Chicago poems.* New York: Henry Holt and Company

Schechter, D. (2003). *Embedded: Weapons of mass deception.* New York: Prometheus.

Schell, J. (1988). *The real war.* New York: Pantheon.

Schemo, D. J. (2006, July 13). Schoolbooks are given F's in originality. *The New York Times.* Retrieved May 1, 2007, from http://be-think.typepad.com/bethink/files/NyTmSchbk.pdf

Schlosser, E. (1998). *The prison-industrial complex.* Retrieved November 16, 2008, from www.theatlantic.com/doc/199812/prisons

Schmitz, D. F. (2005). *The Tet offensive.* New York: Rowman & Littlefield.

School Division of Association of American Publishers. (2009). *AAP School Divison Mission Statement.* Retrieved on January 21, 2009, from www.aapschool.org/aboutus.html

Sewall, G. (2005). Textbook publishing. *Phi Delta Kappan, 86,* 498–502.

Sharp, U. (1979). *Strategy for defeat: Vietnam in retrospect.* San Rafael, CA: Presidio Press.

Sheehan, N. (1988). *A bright shining lie: John Paul Vann and America in Vietnam.* New York: Random House.

Sheehan, N., Butterfield, F., Smith, H., & Kenworthy, E. W. (Eds.). (1971). *The pentagon papers as published by the* New York Times. New York: Quadrangle.

Sleeter, C., & Grant, C. (1991). Race, class, gender, and disability in current textbooks. In M. Apple & L. K. Christian-Smith (Eds.), *The politics of the textbook* (pp. 78–110). New York: Routledge.

Smith, R. (2007). Reed Elsevier's hypocrisy in selling arms and health. *Journal of the Royal Society of Medicine, 100*(3), 114–115.

Sorley, L. (1999). *A better war.* New York: Harcourt Brace & Company.

Spector, R. H. (1993). *After Tet: The bloodiest year in Vietnam.* New York: The Free Press.

Stacewicz, R. (1997). *Winter soldiers: An oral history of the Vietnam veterans against the war.* New York: Twayne Publishers.

Stille, A. (2002, January 29). *Textbook publishers learn: Avoid messing with Texas.* Retrieved on January 7, 2009, from http://query.nytimes.com/gst/fullpage.html?res=9F0CE7DC113EF93AA15755C0A9649C8B63

Stockdale, J., & Stockdale, S. (1984). *In love and war: The story of a family's ordeal and sacrifice during the Vietnam years.* New York: Harper & Row.

Stockholm International Peace Research Institute. (2008). *Recent trends in military spending.* Retrieved July 10, 2008, from www.sipri.org/contents/milap/milex/mex_trends.html

Stokes, R. (1968, September 30). Race riot at Long Binh. *Newsweek, 72*(14), 35.

Summers, H. G. (1984). *On strategy: A critical analysis of the Vietnam War.* New York: Dell.

Terry, W. (1968). Black power in Viet Nam. Racial tensions in the military: September 1968. In M. J. Bates (Ed.), *Reporting Vietnam* (pp. 615–627). New York: Library of America.

Thoman, E., & Jolls, T. (2005). *Literacy for the 21st century.* Retrieved February 28, 2009, from www.medialit.org/pdf/mlk/01_MLKorientation.pdf

Thucydides. (1989). *The Peloponnesian War* (T. Hobbes, Trans.). Chicago: University of Chicago Press. (Original work published 1629)

Troops to Teachers. (2008). *Troops to Teachers Homepage.* Retrieved November 11, 2008, from www.dantes.doded.mil/dantes_Web/troopstoteachers/index2.asp

Tulley, M. A., & Farr, R. (1990). Textbook evaluation and selection. In D. L. Elliott & A. Woodcock (Eds.), *Textbooks and schooling in the United States* (pp. 162–177). Chicago: University of Chicago Press.

Tyson-Bernstein, H. (1988). The academy's contribution to the impoverishment of American textbooks. *Phi Delta Kappan, 70*(3), 192–198.

U.S. Army Recruiting Command. (2006). *Recruiting operations.* Fort Knox, KY: Author.

U.S. Commission on Civil Rights. (1980). *Characters in textbooks: A review of the literature* (Clearing House Publication, Vol. 62). Washington, DC: U.S. Government Printing Office.

U.S. Department of Education, Office of Research and Improvement, National Center for Education Statistics. (2001). *The Nation's report card: U.S. History 2001* (NCES 2002–483). Washington, DC: Author.

U.S. Department of Justice. (2008). *Prison statistics, Summary findings 2007.* Retrieved January 5, 2009, from www.ojp.usdoj.gov/bjs/prisons.htm

Valentine, D. (1990). *The Phoenix program.* New York: William Morrow & Company.

Vinson, K., Gibson, R., & Ross, E. W. (2004). Pursuing authentic education in an age of standardization. In E. W. Ross, D. Gabbard, K. Kesson, & S. Mathison (Eds.), *Defending public schools* (Vol. 2, pp. 83–100). Westport, CT: Praeger.

War and the Smithsonian. (1994, August 29). *Wall Street Journal*, p. A10.

Westmoreland, W. C. (1976). *A soldier reports.* New York: Doubleday.

The White House. (2006). *Joint resolution to authorize the use of United States armed forces against Iraq.* Retrieved January 10, 2006, from www.whitehouse.gov/news/releases/2002/10/20021002-2.html

Williams, R. (1961). *The long revolution.* New York: Columbia University Press.

Willis, P. (1977). *Learning to labor: How working class kids get working class jobs.* Westmead, United Kingdom: Saxon House.

Wills, G. (1992). *Lincoln at Gettysburg.* New York: Simon & Schuster.

Wineburg, S. (2001). *Historical thinking and other unnatural acts.* Philadelphia: Temple University Press.

Wirtz, J. J. (1991a). *The Tet offensive: Intelligence failure in war.* Ithaca, NY: Cornell University Press.

Wirtz, J. J. (1991b). Intelligence to please? The order of battle controversy during the Vietnam War. *Political Science Quarterly, 106*(2), 239–263.

Wood, G. H. (1998). Democracy and the curriculum. In L. E. Beyer & M. W. Apple (Eds.), *The curriculum: Problems, politics, and possibilities* (pp. 177–198). Albany: State University of New York Press.

Woods Jr., A. (2008). *Worshipping the myths of World War II.* Washington, DC: Potomac Books.

Wyatt, C. (1993). *Paper soldiers: The American press and the Vietnam War.* New York: W. W. Norton.

Young, M. (1991). *The Vietnam wars, 1945–1970.* New York: Harper Perennial.

Young, M. J. (1990). Writing and editing textbooks. In D. L. Elliott & A. Woodward (Eds.), *Textbooks and schooling in the United States* (pp. 71–85). Chicago: University of Chicago Press.

Zinn, H. (1967). *The logic of withdrawal.* Boston: Beacon.

Index

About the Author

Christopher R. Leahey teaches world history in upstate New York. His articles have appeared in *Social Education* and *The Social Studies*. In 2003, the Central New York Council for Social Studies recognized him as teacher of the year. In addition to teaching world history and geography, he teaches professional development courses in instructional technology and classroom management. He currently lives in Liverpool, New York, with his wife and three children. He is presently working on a project on democratic teaching methods for history education. Please send inquiries to cleahey1@msn.com